ARISTOTLE

Political & Government Terms & Expressions Explained

Using Analogies Even Young Children Can Easily Understand

This book is dedicated to my two beautiful children,

Isabelle and Ris.

−Aristotle

Contents

1

Introduction For Parents and Educators

Thank you for visiting "Political & Government Terms & Expressions Explained: Using Analogies Even Young Children Can Easily Understand." In this thorough handbook, we set out on a singular quest to make difficult political ideas understandable and interesting for young minds.

It is crucial for kids to have a fundamental understanding of political and governmental structures in the fast changing world of today. However, we recognize that it can be difficult to explain concepts like "suffrage" or "foreign policy" to a 10-year-old. This book was written specifically to bridge the gap between sophisticated vocabulary and kid-friendly analogies.

You hold the key to releasing a child's potential to develop into an informed and active citizen as parents and educators. Our goal is to give you the methods, parallels, and skills you need to decipher political lingo and develop a passion for studying government.

You can find creative analogies and realistic situations that turn vague thoughts into concrete, clear notions throughout these pages. It doesn't matter if you're talking about "voter turnout" or "foreign aid," our goal is to bring these concepts to life in a way that appeals to young learners.

We are aware of how important you are in forming the minds of future generations. This book is here to help you along the way by giving you not only analogies but also useful advice and insights to help you have fruitful discussions with kids about politics and the government.

Join us on this educational journey as we transform political jargon into engrossing tales and governmental jargon into accessible experiences. Together, we can equip young brains to become informed, engaged, and civically responsible.

I appreciate your commitment to developing tomorrow's leaders. Join me as we set out on this educational journey.

2

Introduction For Students and Young Adults

Hey there, awesome young reader!

Welcome to "***Political & Government Terms & Expressions Explained: Using Analogies Even Young Children Can Easily Understand.***" This super cool book is all about helping you learn about politics and government in a fun and easy way.

You might have heard some big words like "politics" and "government" and wondered what they mean. Well, we're here to help! We want to make sure you understand these things because they play a big part in our world.

In this book, we'll explain things using simple words and fun examples that you can relate to. We'll talk about important stuff like how rules are made, how leaders are chosen, and why it all matters to you.

We believe that everyone, including awesome kids like you, can be a part of making our world a better place. And to do that, you need to know how things work! This book is here to help you do just that.

So, whether you're working on a school project, having a chat with friends, or just curious about the world, this book is your go-to guide. It's like having a friendly helper right by your side.

We're so excited to go on this learning adventure with you. Let's get started!

3

Democracy and Governance

Authoritarianism & Totalitarianism

Authoritarianism

Imagine if a teacher in your school made all the rules without asking for anyone's opinion. You'd have to follow those rules even if you didn't agree with them. Authoritarianism is like when leaders in a country have a lot of power and make most of the decisions without listening to what the people want.

Autocracy

Think about a game where one person gets to be the boss and makes all the rules. They don't ask for anyone else's input, and everyone has to do what the boss says. In an autocracy, it's similar. One person, like a king or a queen, has all the power and makes all the important decisions without asking the people.

Censorship

Picture a library where there's a special section that you're not allowed to go into. It's like there's a big curtain blocking it off, and you can't see what's behind it. This is what happens with censorship. Some information or books might be kept away from people, either because the leaders don't want them to know or because they think it's not suitable.

Censorship Laws

Imagine if your school had rules saying certain books or websites were off-limits, even if they weren't harmful. Censorship laws are like those rules, but for a whole country. They're specific rules about what information people can access or share.

Centralized Authority

Think about a big tree with one strong trunk and all the branches growing out from it. The trunk is like the centralized authority, which is the main source of power in a country. It makes most of the important decisions and guides how things are done.

Coup d'État

Picture a group of students trying to take over the playground during recess time, even though it's against the rules. This sudden and forceful takeover is like a coup d'état, where a small group tries to take control of a government.

Cult of Personality

Imagine if a classmate started acting like they were the best at everything, even when they weren't. They might have a big group of followers who believe everything they say. This is similar to a cult of personality, where a leader is praised and followed almost like a superstar, even if they're not always right.

Despotism

Think about a game where one player makes all the rules and doesn't let anyone else have a say. They might even change the rules to favor themselves. Despotism is like when a leader has a lot of power and uses it selfishly, without considering what's fair for everyone.

Dictatorship

Imagine if your class had a substitute teacher who didn't let anyone talk or share their ideas. They decided everything, and nobody could say otherwise. That's a bit like living in a dictatorship, where one person has all the power and makes all the important choices.

Dissident

Picture a group of friends who all want to play a different game, but one friend stands up and says, "Let's play this instead!" That friend is a bit like a dissident. They have a different opinion and are brave enough to speak up, even if it's not the most popular idea.

Martial Law

Think about a special day at school when there's a big event happening, and there are extra rules to make sure everyone stays safe. Martial law is a bit like that, but for a whole city or country. It's when the government puts extra rules in place during a serious situation.

Oligopoly

Imagine a game where only a few players have all the best cards and decide how the game is played. That's like an oligopoly in the business world. It's when just a few big companies have a lot of control over an entire industry.

One-Party System

Think about a school election where only one student is allowed to run for class president, and nobody else can even try. This is a bit like a one-party system in a country. There's only one political group allowed to be in charge, so there's no real choice for the people.

Personality Cult

Imagine if a famous singer came to your school, and suddenly everyone started dressing and acting exactly like them. This is similar to a personality cult, where people admire and copy a leader so much that they almost act like them.

Police State

Picture your school with so many teachers watching every move you make, even during lunch and recess. It might feel a bit like living in a police state, where there's a lot of control and supervision from the government.

Political Oppression

Think about a group project where one person takes charge and doesn't let anyone else have a say. They might even be mean to others who don't agree with them. This is like political oppression, where people who have different ideas are treated unfairly.

Political Repression

Imagine if some students in your class were told they couldn't join clubs or activities just because they had different opinions. This is similar to political repression, where people are kept from expressing their ideas freely.

Propaganda

Picture a friend who tells you a story that's not true, just to make themselves look really good. That's a bit like propaganda, where information is spread to make a certain group or idea seem better than it really is.

Propaganda Machine

Think about a machine that takes in stories and turns them into something completely different. In a way, that's what a propaganda machine does. It takes information and changes it to make people believe a certain way.

Regime

Imagine if your school had a group of older students who made all the rules and didn't listen to what the younger students wanted. This is a bit like a regime, where a small group has a lot of power and control over everyone else.

Regressive Policies

Think about a game where the rules keep changing, and it's always getting harder and less fair for some players. Regressive policies are a bit like that in a country. They're rules that make things more difficult, especially for certain groups of people.

Secret Police

Imagine if there were students at your school who were watching and listening to everything that happened, but you didn't know who they were. This is a bit like having secret police in a country, who work undercover to keep an eye on what people are doing and saying.

State Control

Picture your school deciding what games you can play during recess and who you can play with. In a way, that's what state control is like in a country. The government has a big say in how things are done.

State Surveillance

Think about a big invisible eye in the sky that watches everything you do, even in your own backyard. State surveillance is a bit like that, where the government keeps a close watch on what people are up to.

State-sponsored Media

Imagine if the school newspaper was only allowed to write about things the principal liked, and they couldn't talk about anything else. State-sponsored media is a bit like that, where the government controls what information gets shared with the public.

Suppression of Dissent

Picture a classroom where one student tries to speak up and share their opinion, but the teacher keeps telling them to be quiet. This is like the suppression of dissent, where people who have different ideas are kept from speaking up.

Surveillance State

Think about a school where there are cameras in every hallway and even in the classrooms, watching everything that happens. That's what it's like to live in a surveillance state, where the government keeps a close eye on everyone.

Thought Control

Imagine if there were rules about what you were allowed to think or talk about, even when you were playing with your friends. Thought control is a bit like that, where the government tries to control what people think.

Thought Police

Picture a group of teachers who walk around during recess, listening to what students are saying and making sure they're not talking about certain things. That's a bit like having thought police, who watch what people say and think.

Totalitarianism

Think about a game where one player gets to make all the rules and nobody else has a say. Totalitarianism is like that, but for a whole country. One person or a small group has all the power and makes all the important decisions.

Constitutional Law

Bill of Rights

Imagine if your school had a special list of rules that said everyone has the right to play, learn, and express themselves in certain ways. This list is like the Bill of Rights in a country. It's a set of important rules that protect the freedoms and rights of all the people.

Declaration of Independence

Think of your school as a big clubhouse with different groups of friends. One day, a group of friends might decide they want to have their own clubhouse and make their own rules. This is a bit like what happened when a group of people in a country wrote the Declaration of Independence. They said they wanted to be independent and make their own decisions.

I hope these analogies make the concepts of the Bill of Rights and Declaration of Independence easier to understand for young readers! If you have more terms or need further assistance, feel free to let me know.

Democracy

Civil Liberties

Think of civil liberties like a set of special tools that everyone gets to use to build and create things. These tools help protect your rights to speak freely, worship the way you want, and do other important things.

Democracy

Imagine your class has to decide on a game to play, and everyone gets to vote on which game they like best. The game that most people choose is the one you all play. This is like how a democracy works, where everyone gets a say in important decisions.

Direct Democracy

Picture a class where everyone gets to raise their hand and vote on what game to play next. That's a bit like direct democracy, where everyone has a direct say in the decisions.

Equal Protection Clause

Imagine your teacher making sure that every student gets the same amount of playtime during recess. This is similar to the equal protection clause, which makes sure that everyone is treated fairly and equally under the law.

Free Speech

Think of free speech like having a special pass that lets you express your thoughts and ideas without getting into trouble, as long as you're respectful and kind.

Freedom of the Press

Picture a school newspaper where students can write about different topics and share their ideas. This is like freedom of the press, where people can write and share information without the government stopping them.

Majority Rule

Imagine you and your classmates are trying to decide which game to play, and most of them want to play tag. In a majority rule, you'd play tag because it's what most people want.

Minority Rights

Think of minority rights as special shields that protect the ideas and opinions of students who might have different preferences or thoughts. These shields make sure everyone's voice is heard, even if they're not in the biggest group.

Popular Sovereignty

Imagine a big puzzle with many pieces, and each piece represents a person's opinion. In popular sovereignty, the pieces come together to create a big picture, showing what most people want.

Representative Democracy

Think about a class president election where students vote for a classmate to represent them and make decisions. This is like a representative democracy, where people choose leaders to make decisions on their behalf.

Republic

Imagine if your class decided to have a group of students who help make important decisions for the whole class. This is a bit like a republic, where elected leaders help make decisions for the country.

Rule of Law

Picture your school having a set of rules that everyone follows, even the teachers. The rule of law is a bit like that, where there are fair rules that everyone, even the leaders, must follow.

Supremacy Clause

Think of the supremacy clause as a special rule that says when there's a disagreement between different rules, the most important rule is the one that comes from the highest authority, like the school principal's rules being more important than a classmate's.

Direct Democracy

Referendum

Imagine your class needs to decide on a special day for a fun event, like a big school carnival. Instead of the teachers deciding, they ask all the students to vote on which day they prefer. This is a bit like a referendum, where everyone in a city or country gets to vote on an important decision, like whether to make a new rule or change something big.

Governance

Autonomy

Imagine you have a special box of toys that you get to organize and play with however you like. You can decide which toys go where and how to play with them. Having this control over your toys is a bit like having autonomy, where a group or place can make decisions and rules for themselves.

Citizenship Test

Think of a citizenship test like a big puzzle that you have to solve to become a member of an exclusive club. It has questions about your knowledge and understanding of the rules and values of that club.

Political Instability

Picture a game of Jenga where the blocks keep wobbling and falling over because they're not stacked well. This is a bit like political instability, where a country's leadership and rules might be shaky and not very reliable.

Monarchy & Oligarcy

Absolute Monarchy

Imagine if your school had a king or queen who made all the rules and decisions, and nobody could say otherwise. This is like living in an absolute monarchy, where one person has all the power and control.

Aristocracy

Think of an aristocracy like a special club where only the oldest and richest students get to be members. They make all the important decisions and have a lot of influence over what happens in the school.

Constitutional Monarchy

Picture your school having a principal, but instead of making all the rules by themselves, they have to follow a special book of rules called the "Principal's Guidebook." This is a bit like a constitutional monarchy, where the king or queen follows a set of rules (constitution) that limits their power.

Monarchy

Imagine if your school had a king or queen who made the final decisions about everything, from what games to play at recess to what subjects to study. This is like living in a monarchy, where one person holds a lot of power.

Oligarchy

Think of an oligarchy like a group project where only a few students get to decide what the project will be about and how it will be done. They have a lot of power, and the rest of the class has to go along with their choices.

Plutocracy

Picture a school where the students who have the most toys get to make all the important decisions. They decide what games to play and what activities to do. This is similar to a plutocracy, where the richest people have the most influence over what happens in a country.

4

Political Systems and Ideologies

Capitalism

Capitalism

Imagine your school having a big treasure hunt where everyone can find and collect special coins. These coins are like money, and in a capitalist system, people can buy and sell things using this money.

Competition

Think of a sports day at your school where there are lots of different races and games. Everyone tries their hardest to win because they want to get a special prize. This is like competition in capitalism, where businesses work hard to offer the best products or services so they can attract customers.

Entrepreneurship

Picture a group of friends who start a lemonade stand together. They come up with the idea, gather the ingredients, and sell the lemonade. This is a bit like entrepreneurship, where people come up with their own ideas for businesses and work hard to make them successful.

Free Market

Imagine if your school had a big swap meet where students could bring toys, books, or even snacks to trade with each other. This is like a free market, where people can buy and sell things without too many rules or restrictions.

Meritocracy

Think about a school talent show where the students who practice the most and perform the best get special awards. This is like a meritocracy, where people get rewarded based on their hard work and skills.

Political Economy

Picture your school as a big treehouse where students have to trade snacks, toys, and favors with each other. This is like a political economy, where people in a country have to figure out how to share and trade resources.

Private Ownership

Imagine if you had a special box of toys that only you could play with, and you could decide what to do with them. This is like private ownership, where individuals or companies own things like land, businesses, or houses.

Supply and Demand

Think of your school's lunchtime snacks. When there are only a few cookies left, but lots of students want them, the price might go up (maybe it costs more than one snack coupon). When there are plenty of apples, they might be cheaper. This is like supply and demand in capitalism, where the price of things can change based on how much there is and how many people want it.

Environmentalism

Green Politics

Imagine your school deciding to have a special day where everyone works together to plant new trees, take care of plants, and make the schoolyard a more beautiful and natural place. Green politics is a bit like this special day, but for a whole community or even a country. It's about making decisions and rules that help protect the environment and keep our planet healthy and green.

Liberalism, Conservatism, and Fascism

Conservatism

Think about your favorite stuffed animal or toy. You really like it just the way it is and don't want to change it. You want to keep it the same because you like it that way. This feeling is a bit like conservatism in politics. It's about wanting to keep things the way they are, without making big changes.

Factionalism

Imagine if your class was trying to decide on a game to play, but everyone had a different favorite. Some wanted tag, others wanted soccer, and a few liked hide-and-seek. It's like there are little groups, or factions, with their own ideas. In politics, factionalism happens when different groups have their own strong opinions about how things should be done.

Fascism

Picture a game where one person makes all the rules, and nobody else can say anything. This person gets to decide everything, and everyone has to follow along. This is like living under a fascist government, where one person or group has all the power and control.

Individual Rights

Imagine if everyone in your class had a special badge that showed they could choose what game to play at recess. This badge means they have the right to decide. Individual rights are a bit like these special badges, giving people the freedom to make choices for themselves.

Liberalism

Think about a big art project where everyone gets to pick what colors to use and what shapes to make. It's about expressing your own ideas and being creative. This is a bit like liberalism in politics. It's about giving people the freedom to express themselves and make choices for themselves.

Libertarianism

Picture a school where students have a lot of freedom to choose what games to play, when to have lunch, and even what subjects to study. In a way, this is a bit like libertarianism in politics. It's about having a lot of personal freedom and making choices for yourself.

Nationalism

Imagine your school cheering for your sports team against another school. Everyone is waving flags, wearing team colors, and showing lots of school spirit. This feeling of pride and support is a bit like nationalism in politics.

It's when people have a strong love and loyalty for their own country.

Political Extremism

Think about a game where some students want to play super seriously and others just want to have fun. When people have really strong and sometimes extreme opinions about how things should be done, it's a bit like political extremism. It means they're very passionate about their beliefs.

Tradition

Picture a special family dinner where everyone makes a favorite dish, just like they do every year. This tradition is something that's done the same way, year after year. In politics, tradition is about valuing and keeping important customs and practices that have been followed for a long time.

Socialism, Communism, etc.

Collective Ownership

Imagine if your class decided to build a big treehouse together. Everyone contributed something, like wood, nails, and paint. When it's done, everyone can use it and share it equally. This is a bit like collective ownership, where everyone in a community owns and uses things together.

Communism

Think about a game where everyone gets the same number of toys and snacks, no matter what. Nobody has more or less than anyone else. This is a bit like how communism works, where everyone in a community shares things equally.

Equality

Picture a game where all the players have the same chances to win. Nobody has an advantage or a head start. This is what equality means - making sure everyone has a fair shot at success.

Planned Economy

Imagine your class planning a big party together. Everyone decides what snacks to bring, what games to play, and how to decorate. This is a bit like a planned economy, where the government helps decide what goods and services should be produced.

Redistribution of Wealth

Think of a game where everyone starts with the same number of tokens, but some people might win more while others lose some. At the end of the game, everyone shares their tokens so that everyone has about the same. This is like the redistribution of wealth, making sure that everyone has a fair amount of resources.

Socialism

Picture a class where everyone helps each other out. If someone forgets their lunch, others share theirs. If someone needs help with homework, others lend a hand. This is a bit like socialism, where people in a community work together to support each other.

Tyranny

Picture a school where one student becomes the boss and makes all the rules, even the ones that don't seem fair. This student doesn't listen to others and decides everything without caring about what everyone else thinks. That's a bit like tyranny – when one person has too much power and doesn't let others have a say in how things should be done. It's like having a bossy classmate who forgets that everyone's opinions matter.

5

Institutions of Government

Archives and Records Management

Government Archivist

Imagine your school has a special team of students whose job is to collect and take care of all the important memories and records from every school year. They keep everything organized so that everyone can look back and see what happened in the past. A government archivist is like the head of this special team for a whole country. They take care of important documents and records to make sure the country's history is remembered and preserved.

Constitutional Law

Constitutional Convention

Imagine your school is like a big treehouse, and every year, students gather to talk about and decide on important rules for the treehouse. They might discuss things like what games are allowed, how to share snacks, and how to resolve disagreements. This special meeting where everyone comes together to make important decisions is a bit like a Constitutional Convention. It's a big event where people gather to talk about and decide on the important rules for a whole country.

I hope this analogy helps in understanding what a Constitutional Convention is! If you have more terms or need further assistance, feel free to let me know.

Executive Branch

Administrative Law

Think of administrative law as the rulebook your class follows for special projects. It tells you how things should be done, like who's in charge of what, and how to make sure everything runs smoothly.

Attorney General

Pretend your school has a super detective who helps solve any mysteries or problems that come up. This person is like an attorney general, but instead of solving school mysteries, they help figure out legal issues for the whole country.

Cabinet

Imagine if your class had a group of special experts for different subjects, like a math expert, a science expert, and a history expert. They would help the teacher make important decisions about what to learn. This group of experts is a bit like a cabinet, which helps the leader of a country make important decisions about different areas, like education, health, and more.

Central Intelligence Agency (CIA)

Think of the CIA as a group of secret agents who work to keep your school safe. They gather important information and help make sure everyone is secure and protected.

Chief of Staff

Let's say your school has a super-organized student who helps the teacher with important tasks, like making sure everyone has the right books and supplies. This student is like a chief of staff, who helps the leader of a country stay organized and make sure everything runs smoothly.

Commander-in-Chief

Pretend your school has a super captain who's in charge of all the games during recess. They make sure everyone plays fair and that everything is safe. In the same way, a commander-in-chief is like the captain of the whole country, in charge of making sure everyone is safe and protected.

Director of National Intelligence

Imagine your school has a student who's really, really good at solving puzzles and figuring things out. They're like a detective who helps the teacher understand what's going on. The director of national intelligence is a bit like this puzzle-solving expert, but for the whole country.

Environmental Protection Agency (EPA)

Think of the EPA as a special team of nature superheroes who make sure your school's garden and playground stay clean and healthy. They work to protect the environment and keep it safe for everyone.

Ethics Commissioner

Pretend your school has a fairness expert who makes sure that everyone is treated equally and no one is left out. This person is like an ethics commissioner, who helps make sure that people in the government act fairly and follow the rules.

Executive Branch

Let's say your school is like a big ship, and there's one student who's the captain, making sure everything goes smoothly. The captain is a bit like the executive branch, which is in charge of running the whole country.

Federal Bureau of Investigation (FBI)

Imagine if your school had a group of super detectives who helped keep everyone safe and made sure nobody broke the rules. They investigate any mysteries or problems that come up. This group is a bit like the FBI, which helps keep the whole country safe.

Governor

Think of a governor as the head student in charge of a big school district. They make important decisions for all the schools in the area, like setting rules and making sure everyone gets what they need.

Head of Government

Pretend your school has a special leader who's really good at making decisions and organizing events. They help make sure everything runs smoothly and everyone is happy. This person is like the head of government, who helps lead and make decisions for the whole country.

Head of State

Imagine your school has a special representative who welcomes guests and makes sure everyone feels welcome and included. This person is like the head of state, who represents the country and helps make sure everyone is treated well.

Immunity from Prosecution

Let's say there's a game where everyone has special shields that make them immune to getting tagged. They can play without worrying about getting out. Immunity from prosecution is a bit like having a special shield that protects someone from being punished for something they did.

Inherent Powers

Think of inherent powers like a super skill that some students have. For example, some are really good at drawing, while others are great at running. In the same way, inherent powers are special skills and abilities that the leader of a country has naturally.

Inspector General

Pretend your school has a special super-spy who checks to make sure everything is safe and fair. They make sure that everyone follows the rules and that nobody is doing anything sneaky. An inspector general is like this super-spy for the whole country.

Lame Duck Period

Imagine a game where some players are about to leave, but they still get to play for a little while before they go. They're like "lame ducks" because they're not staying for long, but they still get to participate.

National Security Agency (NSA)

Think of the NSA as a group of super-secret agents who are really good at listening and watching to make sure everyone stays safe. They work behind the scenes to protect the country.

Ombudsman

Pretend your school has a special helper who listens to any problems or complaints students might have. They make sure everyone's voice is heard and help find solutions. An ombudsman is like this special helper for the whole country.

Pardon

Imagine a game where if someone accidentally breaks a rule, they can say "sorry" and keep playing. A pardon is a bit like saying "sorry" in a game. It's when the leader forgives someone for breaking a rule and they don't get in trouble.

President

Let's say your school is like a big ship, and there's one student who's the captain, making sure everything goes smoothly. This student is like the president, who is in charge of running the whole country.

Prime Minister

Think of a prime minister as the head student who helps the teacher make important decisions for the class. They work together to make sure everyone has what they need and that everything runs smoothly.

Secret Service

Imagine if your school had a special team of superguards who protected important guests and made sure nobody unwanted came in. They work behind the scenes to keep everyone safe.

Secretaries (of various departments)

Picture each secretary as a specialist in charge of a different subject, like a math expert, a science expert, and a history expert. They help the leader of the country make important decisions about different areas, like education, health, and more.

Veto Power

Think of veto power as a special stop sign that the leader can hold up to stop a decision from being made. It's like saying "wait, let's think about this a little more" before something becomes a rule.

Vice President

Imagine your school has a helper who's always there to support the captain, making sure everything runs smoothly. This person is like the vice president, who helps the president with important tasks.

War Powers Resolution

Think of the War Powers Resolution like a special rule in a game. It says that if something really serious happens, everyone needs to stop and talk about it before taking any big actions. It's like having a timeout to make sure everyone agrees on what to do.

Judicial Branch

Chief Justice

Pretend your class is like a big puzzle, and the chief justice is the student who's really good at putting all the pieces together. They make sure everything fits just right.

Courts

Think of courts like different game arenas at a playground. Each arena has its own set of rules and games. Just like you go to different places to play different games, people go to different courts to solve different kinds of problems.

Federal Judge

Imagine your school has a super wise owl who helps settle disputes and makes sure everyone is treated fairly. A federal judge is like this wise owl, but they help settle disputes for the whole country.

Interpretation of Laws

Pretend your class is reading a really exciting story, but everyone has their own idea of what the characters look like and how the scenes play out. Interpretation of laws is a bit like this - different people might see and understand the rules in different ways.

Judges

Let's say your class is like a big team of superheroes, and each one has a special power. Judges are like the superheroes who help make important decisions and keep everything fair.

Judicial Activism

Think of judicial activism like a referee in a game who isn't afraid to blow the whistle when they see something wrong. They make sure everyone follows the rules and plays fair.

Judicial Branch

Imagine your school is like a big treehouse, and there's a special area where students gather to talk about and solve problems. This area is a bit like the judicial branch, where important decisions are made to make sure everyone is treated fairly.

Judicial Independence

Pretend your school has a group of students who are really good at thinking for themselves and making fair decisions. They don't let others tell them what to do. This is a bit like judicial independence, where judges make decisions based on what they believe is right, not what someone else tells them to do.

Judicial Nomination

Let's say your class needs to choose a leader for a special project. Each student gets to nominate someone they think would do a great job. The process of choosing the leader is a bit like judicial nomination, where someone is chosen to be a judge.

Judicial Precedent

Imagine your class is like a big book club, and you're all reading the same book. If someone in the club talks about a part of the book that everyone agrees is really important, it becomes a special reference point. Judicial precedent is a bit like this - it's a past decision that helps guide future decisions.

Judicial Review

Think of judicial review like a special magnifying glass that helps you see things more clearly. It's a process that helps make sure laws are fair and follow the rules.

Justice

Imagine a big scale where you put equal amounts of things on both sides to make sure everything is fair. This is a bit like justice, where decisions are made to make sure everyone is treated equally and fairly.

Plea Bargain

Pretend you and a friend have a disagreement about which game to play. Instead of arguing, you both agree to play one game for a while, then switch to the other. This is a bit like a plea bargain, where people agree to a fair solution instead of going through a long process.

Public Defender

Think of a public defender like a superhero lawyer who helps people who might not have their own lawyer. They make sure everyone gets a fair chance.

Supreme Court

Imagine your school has a special council of super wise students who make the most important decisions about rules and projects. This council is like the supreme court, which makes the most important decisions about the laws of the whole country.

Legislative Branch

Auditor General

Pretend your school has a super detective who checks all the financial records to make sure everything adds up and no money is missing. The auditor general is like this super detective, but for the whole country.

Bicameral Legislature

Think of a bicameral legislature like a big puzzle that's split into two parts. Each part has its own set of pieces, and together they make a complete picture. Just like you need both parts to complete the puzzle, a country needs both parts of a bicameral legislature to make important decisions.

Chaplain of the Senate

Imagine your school has a wise and caring guardian who offers support and kind words to everyone. The chaplain of the Senate is like this guardian, offering support and encouragement to the members of the Senate.

Clerk of the House

Think of the clerk of the house as the master organizer in a big library. They make sure all the books (or in this case, important documents) are in the right place and easy to find.

Comptroller General

Pretend your school has a super organizer who keeps track of everything - from books to supplies to events. They make sure everything is accounted for and in the right place. The comptroller general does something similar, but for the whole country.

Congress

Let's say your school is like a big meeting place where everyone gets together to talk about important things. This meeting place is a bit like Congress, where important decisions are made for the whole country.

Congressional Aide

Imagine your school has a special helper who supports the teacher and makes sure everything is running smoothly. They help with important tasks and make sure everything is in order. This helper is like a congressional aide, who supports the members of Congress.

Constituency

Think of a constituency like your group of close friends. They're the people you know and care about the most. In the same way, a constituency is the group of people a representative in Congress cares for and represents.

Dissolution of Parliament

Let's say your class is working on a big project, but when the project is finished, you decide to take a break and start something new. This is a bit like the dissolution of parliament, when one period of work ends and a new one begins.

Doorkeeper

Imagine your school has a friendly student who stands at the entrance, greeting everyone and making sure only authorized people come in. They're like the doorkeeper, who helps control who enters the legislative building.

Electoral Commission

Think of an electoral commission like a team of referees in a game. They make sure the game is fair and everyone follows the rules. The electoral commission ensures that elections are fair and everyone's vote counts.

Filibuster

Pretend you and your friends are playing a game, and one friend keeps talking and talking to delay the game. This friend is doing something like a filibuster, where someone talks for a long time to delay a decision in Congress.

House Historian

Imagine your school has a special expert who knows everything about the school's history. They can tell you about the important events and people from the past. The house historian is like this expert, but for the House of Representatives.

House of Representatives

Think of the House of Representatives like a big team where each player represents a different group. Together, they work to make important decisions for everyone.

Impeachment

Pretend there's a special process in your class where, if someone isn't following the rules, the teacher holds a meeting to decide what to do. This meeting is a bit like impeachment, where a decision is made about whether someone should be removed from their position.

Joint Resolution

Think of a joint resolution like a special agreement that everyone in your class signs to say they agree on something important. It's a way for everyone to come together and make a decision.

Lawmaking

Imagine your class is like a big team of detectives, and you're all trying to solve a mystery. Together, you work to figure out what's right and what should be done. Lawmaking is a bit like this, where people work together to create rules for the whole country.

Legislative Oversight

Let's say your class is working on a big project, and the teacher checks in to make sure everything is going smoothly. This is a bit like legislative oversight, where Congress checks to make sure everything in the government is working well.

No-Confidence Vote

Imagine if your class could hold a special vote to express how confident they are in a project's success. A no-confidence vote is like saying, "We don't think this is going to work, so let's try something else."

Parliament

Think of parliament like a big school assembly where everyone comes together to talk about important things and make decisions for the whole school.

Parliamentary Budget Officer

Pretend your class has a special math expert who helps plan how to spend money on important projects. They make sure everything adds up and is used wisely. The parliamentary budget officer does something similar for the whole country.

Parliamentary Counsel

Think of parliamentary counsel like a team of language experts who make sure all the rules and documents are clear and easy to understand.

Parliamentary Librarian

Imagine your school has a special expert who knows everything about books and helps everyone find the information they need. The parliamentary librarian is like this expert, but for the parliament.

Parliamentary Procedure

Think of parliamentary procedure like a set of special rules everyone agrees to follow during a big meeting. These rules help make sure everyone's voice is heard and decisions are made fairly.

Quorum

Pretend your class is working on a project, and you need at least a certain number of students to be there to make decisions. This minimum number of students is like a quorum, which is the minimum number of people needed to make decisions in Congress.

Ratification Process

Imagine your class creates a special club, but before it officially starts, everyone needs to agree on some important rules. The process of agreeing on these rules is a bit like the ratification process, where everyone agrees on important decisions.

Senate

Think of the Senate like a team of expert advisors who help make important decisions for the whole country.

Senate Historian

Imagine your school has a special expert who knows everything about the history of your school's student council. They can tell you about important events and decisions from the past. The Senate historian is like this expert, but for the Senate.

Senate Majority Leader

Think of the Senate majority leader as the student who helps organize all the student council meetings and make sure everything runs smoothly.

Sergeant-at-Arms

Imagine your school has a superhero guard who makes sure everyone is safe and follows the rules during important meetings. They help maintain order and make sure everything runs smoothly.

Speaker of the House

Think of the speaker of the house as the head student who leads important meetings and makes sure everyone has a chance to speak and be heard.

Whip

Imagine your class is working on a big project, and there's a student who helps keep everyone on track and makes sure everything is moving forward. This student is like a whip, who helps members of Congress stay organized and make progress.

Local Government

City Council Member

Pretend that your class is like a team of superheroes, and each member has a special power that helps the class. A city council member is like a superhero for your city, and their special power is making important decisions to help the community.

County Commissioner

Let's say your school is like a big puzzle with many pieces. Each piece represents a different area, like a classroom or a play area. The county commissioner is like the student who helps put all the pieces together and make sure everything fits just right.

Mayor

Think of your city as a big treehouse, and the mayor is like the head treehouse keeper. They make sure everything in the treehouse is running smoothly, and they listen to the ideas and concerns of all the treehouse members.

Separation of Powers

Checks and Balances

Let's say your class is working on a big art project together. There are different roles: painters, organizers, and decorators. If one group does too much or makes all the decisions, the project might not turn out as great. So, you have a system where everyone checks on each other's work to make sure everything is balanced and looks amazing in the end. This way, no one group has too much power, and the project comes out just right.

In the same way, in a government, there are different branches, like painters, organizers, and decorators (but in terms of making and enforcing laws). They all have a role, and they keep an eye on each other's work to make sure everything is fair and balanced for the whole country. This system of checks and balances helps ensure that no one branch has too much power and that everything runs smoothly.

State Government

State Representative

Let's say your school has a special team of students who are really good at speaking up for what they believe is right. They listen to everyone's ideas and then stand up to share them with the class. These students are like state representatives. They listen to the ideas and concerns of people in their state, and then they speak up for them in a special meeting.

State Senator 43

Imagine your school has a group of students who are like the wise advisors to the teacher. They help make important decisions about rules and activities. These students are like state senators. They work together to make important decisions for the state, just like your advisors help with decisions for your class.

6

Elections and Political Participation

Electoral Systems and Political Parties

Campaign Finance Reform

Pretend your class is organizing a big event, like a carnival. You want to make sure everyone has a chance to contribute to make it fun. Campaign finance reform is like making sure everyone has an equal chance to bring something cool to the event, so it's enjoyable for everyone.

Caucus

Let's say your class wants to decide on a special activity, like a field trip. Instead of everyone talking at once, you split into small groups to discuss ideas. Each group then chooses a representative to share their group's favorite idea with the whole class. A caucus is like this process, where groups of people discuss and then choose representatives to make decisions.

Election Fraud

Imagine your class is having a contest, and one person tries to sneak in extra votes for themselves. That wouldn't be fair, right? Election fraud is when someone tries to cheat in an election, like adding extra votes or doing something sneaky to win unfairly.

Election Observation

Pretend your class is having a spelling bee, and there's a special judge to make sure everyone follows the rules. This judge is like an election observer, making sure everything is fair and everyone plays by the rules during an election.

Electoral College

Think of your class as a big team trying to solve a puzzle together. The puzzle has different pieces, and each piece represents a point. When you finish a piece, you get a point. The more pieces a state has, the more points it gives. The electoral college is like a special scoring system that helps decide who wins, based on the total points from all the states.

Electoral Fraud

Pretend your class is having a drawing contest, and one person tries to sneak in extra drawings to win. That wouldn't be fair, right? Electoral fraud is when someone tries to cheat in the electoral process, like adding extra votes or doing something sneaky to change the outcome.

Electoral Systems

Think of electoral systems like different games you can play during recess. Each game has its own rules and way of picking a winner. In the same way, different electoral systems have their own rules for how votes are counted and winners are chosen.

First-Past-The-Post

Imagine your class is choosing a class representative, and the student with the most votes wins, even if they don't get more than half of the votes. This is like first-past-the-post, where the candidate with the most votes wins, even if they don't have over 50%.

Gerrymandering

Let's say your class is playing a game of tag, and one student changes the boundaries of the play area to make it easier for them to win. Gerrymandering is like that, where people change the boundaries of voting districts to try to get an advantage for their party.

Impeachment

Think of a special kind of school meeting where students decide if one of their classmates who has been misbehaving a lot should still be allowed to be a class leader. It's like a serious talk about whether that student should keep their important job or not. This is a bit like impeachment in the world of politics – it's a process where people decide if an important leader, like the president, should continue doing their job or if they need to step down because they did something wrong. It's like giving someone a timeout from being in charge until things are sorted out. Impeachment is a way to make sure leaders play fair and follow the rules.

Multi-Party System

Think of a multi-party system like a big pizza party where there are lots of different types of pizza to choose from. Each type of pizza represents a different party, and everyone can pick their favorite. In a multi-party system, there are many different parties to choose from in an election.

Party Platform

Imagine your class is planning a big party, and each student has a different idea for games, food, and decorations. Each student's ideas represent a different part of the party platform. The party platform is like a collection of ideas and goals that a political party believes in.

Plurality Voting

Pretend your class is choosing a favorite book to read, and everyone writes down their top choice. The book with the most votes is the winner, even if it doesn't have more than half the votes. This is like plurality voting, where the option with the most votes wins, even if it doesn't have over 50%.

Political Action Committee (PAC)

Think of a PAC like a group of students who work together to support a cause they all believe in. They might pool their resources and ideas to make a bigger impact. A political action committee is like this group, but for adults who want to support a particular cause or candidate.

Political Parties

Imagine your class divides into different groups, each with its own idea for how to make the school better. These groups are like political parties, which are made up of people who have similar ideas about how to run the country.

Poll

Think of a poll like asking your classmates which ice cream flavor is their favorite. You collect everyone's choices to find out the most popular flavor. In elections, a poll is a bit like that – people ask questions to find out which candidate is the most popular.

Polling

Now, imagine you want to know if your class prefers pizza or burgers for lunch. You ask a few friends, but you can't ask everyone. Polling is when you gather opinions from a small group (like your friends) to make an educated guess about what everyone thinks. It's like figuring out the class lunch favorite without asking every single student.

Primaries

In a school talent show, students audition to be the lead singer for the upcoming concert. Think of primaries as these auditions. Candidates show their skills, and everyone votes to decide who gets the starring role.

Proportional Representation

Let's say your class is choosing a theme for a party, and everyone votes for their favorite. The theme with the most votes is picked, but there's also a fair system where other popular themes get a say too. Proportional representation is like this, where different groups get representation based on how many people support them.

Proxy Voting

Imagine your class is having a vote on a day when some students are absent. These absent students can ask a trusted friend to vote for them. This is like proxy voting, where someone votes on behalf of another person who can't be there.

Public Opinion Poll

Pretend you're doing a survey in your class to find out what everyone's favorite subject is. You ask everyone and record their answers. A public opinion poll is like a big survey for a whole country to find out what people think about important topics.

Redistricting

Think of redistricting like rearranging desks in your classroom. Sometimes, you need to change the arrangement to make sure everyone has a fair and equal seat. In redistricting, boundaries are adjusted to make sure everyone's vote counts equally.

Secret Ballot

Imagine your class is voting on a surprise party theme, and you want your choice to be a secret. You write down your choice on a piece of paper and put it in a box. This way, no one knows who voted for what. A secret ballot is like this, where your vote is private, and no one knows who you voted for.

Swing States

Picture a giant swing on a playground. When some kids want to push it higher, they have to work together to make it swing back and forth. In elections, swing states are a bit like that swing – they can go back and forth, sometimes supporting one side and sometimes the other. Everyone watches these states because they can decide the whole election, just like those kids deciding how high the swing goes!

Two-Party System

Think of a two-party system like a school where there are two main clubs - one for soccer lovers and one for art enthusiasts. Most students join one of these two clubs. In a two-party system, most people align with one of the two main political parties.

Voting Booth

Imagine your class sets up a special area with curtains where students can go to cast their votes during a class election. This private space is like a voting booth, where people can make their choices in secret.

Lobbying and Interest Groups

Advocacy

Think of advocacy like being a spokesperson for a really awesome new game. You love it so much that you tell everyone how great it is and why they should play it too. Advocacy is when people speak up and tell others why something is important and worth supporting.

Grassroots Campaigns

Pretend you're part of a big gardening club, and you all want to make your school's garden the best it can be. Each member works on a small part, like planting flowers or building benches. Together, all your small efforts make the garden amazing. Grassroots campaigns are like this, where lots of regular people work together on small tasks to achieve something big.

Influence

Imagine you're the leader of a dance group, and you come up with a really cool dance move. When you show it to the others, they love it and want to do it too. Your idea had an influence on the whole group. Influence is when your ideas or actions affect and inspire others.

Interest Groups

Think of interest groups like clubs at school. Some students really love science, so they join the Science Club. Others might be passionate about helping animals, so they join the Animal Rights Club. Interest groups are like special clubs for people who care about the same things and want to make a difference.

Lobbying

Pretend you and your friends are trying to convince your teacher to have a special pizza party. You all talk to the teacher, share your reasons, and try to persuade them. Lobbying is like this, but for grown-ups. It's when people try to persuade lawmakers to make certain decisions or support certain ideas.

Lobbying Disclosure

Imagine if your school had a special chart where every time a student talked to a teacher about something important, they wrote it down. This way, everyone knows who talked to whom. Lobbying disclosure is like this chart, but for grown-ups who talk to lawmakers.

Lobbyist

Think of a lobbyist like a messenger in a castle. They're the ones who carry important messages from different people to the king or queen. In the same way, a lobbyist is someone who carries important messages from groups or individuals to lawmakers.

Special Interests

Pretend your school has a group of students who are really passionate about a certain topic, like space exploration. They meet, share ideas, and try to make things happen. These students have a special interest in space. In the same way, special interests are groups of people who are really passionate about a particular cause or idea.

Suffrage

Civic Duty

Pretend that being a member of your class is like being a superhero. Every superhero has a duty to protect their city and help others. In the same way, being a responsible citizen means you have a duty to your community to vote and participate in making decisions.

Mandatory Voting

Let's say your class is planning a fun event, like a field trip, and everyone has to vote on where to go. It's mandatory, which means everyone has to vote because it's important for everyone to have a say. Mandatory voting is like when everyone has to participate and vote in important decisions for the community.

Political Franchise

Think of the political franchise like being part of a special club. This club is for citizens who have the right to vote and help make important decisions for the community. Just like being a member of a club gives you certain privileges, having the political franchise gives you the right to vote.

Suffrage

Pretend your class is making a big decision, like choosing the theme for the school dance. Everyone gets to vote on their favorite theme. Suffrage is like having the right to raise your hand and vote for what you believe in.

Universal Suffrage

Imagine if your school had a rule that said every student, no matter their grade or age, gets to vote on important decisions. Universal suffrage is like this rule, but for a whole country. It means that every citizen, regardless of background or circumstance, has the right to vote.

Voter ID Laws

Let's say your class is having a special party, and to get in, everyone needs to show a special pass with their picture on it. Voter ID laws are like having a special pass (like a school ID) to show that you're eligible to vote.

Voter Intimidation

Pretend you and your friends are playing a game, but some students are trying to scare others so they won't play. That's not fair, right? Voter intimidation is when someone tries to scare or bully people to stop them from voting. It's important that everyone feels safe and free to vote.

Voter Registration

Think of voter registration like signing up for a really fun after-school club. You fill out a form, and then you're officially a member. With voter registration, you fill out a form to become an official member of the voting community.

Voter Suppression

Imagine you and your classmates are playing a game, but some students are making it really hard for others to join or play. Voter suppression is like when people try to make it difficult for certain groups to vote. It's important that everyone has an equal chance to participate.

Voter Turnout

Pretend your class is having a special show, and you want as many students as possible to come watch. The more students who come, the better the show will be. Voter turnout is like this - the more people who come out to vote, the stronger and more representative the decision will be.

Voting Rights

Think of voting rights like having a special key that lets you open a door to a room filled with decisions. Just like a key gives you access, having voting rights gives you the power to participate in making important choices for your community.

Technology in Politics

Blockchain Voting

Let's say you and your friends are building a really big tower out of colorful blocks. Each block has a special code on it to make sure it fits perfectly with the others. Once you add a block, it's locked in place and can't be changed. Blockchain voting is like this tower, but for votes. Each vote is like a block with a special code, and once it's added, it's locked in and can't be altered. This makes sure that the votes are secure and accurate.

This way, everyone can trust that the votes are counted correctly, just like you can trust that your tower is strong and won't fall down!

7

International Relations and Diplomacy

Diplomacy

Ambassador

Pretend you have a special friend in another school who helps make friends and solve problems between different classes. This friend is like an ambassador because they work to build good relationships and understanding between your class and the other one. In the same way, an ambassador in politics is like a special person chosen to represent their country and build good relationships with other countries.

Just like your friend is really good at listening and talking to others, ambassadors are skilled at communicating and finding solutions between different countries. They're like super-friendly peacemakers!

Foreign Policy

Alliances

Think of alliances like your group of close friends. You trust them, and you all work together to help and support each other. Alliances in foreign policy are like when countries become close friends and agree to help each other out in times of need.

Diplomacy

Pretend you and your friends have a disagreement about which game to play. Instead of arguing, you talk calmly and find a game that everyone enjoys. That's a bit like diplomacy - it's about finding peaceful solutions to problems between countries by talking and understanding each other.

Foreign Policy

Let's say your school has a set of rules for how students should behave. Those rules help make sure everyone is treated fairly and kindly. Foreign policy is like a set of rules that a country follows to treat other countries fairly and work together peacefully.

International Relations

Think of international relations like making friends with students from different schools. You learn about their interests, share your own, and find common ground. International relations are about countries getting to know each other, finding common interests, and working together.

Neutrality

Imagine your class is having a big game of soccer, and you're the referee. Your job is to make sure everyone plays fair and doesn't take sides. Neutrality in foreign policy is like being a fair referee between countries. It means not picking sides and working to find solutions that are fair for everyone.

Sovereignty

Pretend you have your own special corner in the classroom where you keep your favorite books and toys. That corner is your space, and you get to decide what goes there. Sovereignty is like that, but for countries. It means they have their own space and get to make their own decisions without others telling them what to do.

Global Security

Nuclear Proliferation

Let's say you have a really special toy that you love and take very good care of. Now, imagine if everyone in the neighborhood wanted a toy just like yours, and they all started making their own. Suddenly, there are many of these special toys around. This is a bit like nuclear proliferation, where different countries start making their own powerful toys, except in this case, it's not toys, but very powerful weapons.

Just like you'd want to make sure your special toy stays safe, countries work together to make sure that these powerful weapons don't get into the wrong hands or cause harm.

Globalization

Imperialism

Let's say you have a big garden, and you really love growing different kinds of fruits and vegetables. You take care of it, water the plants, and make sure everything grows well. Now, imagine if you wanted to help your friends have awesome gardens too, so you start helping them with their gardens. Imperialism is a bit like this, but with countries. It's when one country wants to spread its influence and help other countries grow and develop.

Just like you'd share your gardening tips and tricks with your friends, imperialist countries may try to share their ideas, culture, or resources with other nations.

International Law

International Court of Justice

Think of the International Court of Justice like a big referee at a sports game. In a game, if there's a disagreement about the rules or someone playing unfairly, the referee steps in to make a fair decision. The International Court of Justice does something similar, but for countries. When countries have disagreements or problems, this special "referee" helps make fair decisions.

Jus Cogens

Pretend there's a set of super important rules at school that everyone has to follow. These rules are so important that they're like the superpowers of rules! Jus Cogens are like these super important rules in the world of countries. They're rules that everyone agrees are really, really crucial and can't be ignored.

War Crimes Tribunal

Imagine there's a special court just for deciding if someone did something really, really wrong during a game. Like, if a player was playing really unfairly or hurting others. A War Crimes Tribunal is like this special court, but for grown-ups and very serious situations. It's a place where they decide if someone did something really wrong during a big, grown-up "game" called war.

International Organizations

International Organization

Think of an international organization like a big clubhouse where kids from different neighborhoods come together to play games, share toys, and have fun. In the same way, an international organization is like a special group where countries from around the world come together to work together on important projects and help each other out.

Supranational Organization

Pretend there's a super-duper team of superheroes who join forces to tackle really big problems that no single superhero can solve alone. This team is so strong because they work together and share their special powers. A supranational organization is like a team of countries who join together to solve really big problems that affect them all. They combine their strengths to make a bigger impact.

Isolationism and Globalization

Cultural Exchange

Pretend your school has a special day where students from different grades teach each other about their favorite hobbies and games. You get to learn new things and make new friends. Cultural exchange in the world is like this special day, but for countries. They share their traditions, music, food, and more to learn from one another.

Economic Interdependence

Imagine you and your friends are working together to build an awesome treehouse. Each friend has a special job, like building walls or painting. You all depend on each other to finish the treehouse. Economic interdependence between countries is like this. They work together and rely on each other for things like trading goods, which helps them all prosper.

Globalization

Let's say you have a magical notebook that can connect you to students all around the world. You can share stories, learn about their lives, and even exchange cool drawings. Globalization is a bit like this magical notebook, but for countries. It's when countries connect, share ideas, and work together on things that benefit everyone.

International Organizations

Think of international organizations like a group of really smart grown-ups who want to make the world a better place. They work together, share ideas, and come up with plans to help countries solve big problems. In a way, they're like the superheroes of world problem-solving!

Isolationism

Pretend you have a special fort in your backyard where you and your close friends like to play. Sometimes, you might want to play just with them and not let others join. Isolationism is a bit like this. It's when a country wants to focus on itself and not get too involved with other countries' games or projects.

Trade Agreements

Imagine trading your extra puzzle pieces with a friend who loves puzzles too. You both get what you want and everyone's happy! Trade agreements between countries are like this, but on a much bigger scale. They make deals so that each country gets things they need and want, making everyone better off.

Political Theory

International Relations Theory

Think of international relations theory like different ways people explain why friends get along or sometimes have disagreements. Some say it's because they have similar interests, while others say it's because they help each other out. International relations theory is like these explanations, but for why countries around the world work together or sometimes have disagreements. It helps us understand the big picture of how countries interact with one another.

Just like understanding why friends get along helps you have better friend-ships, understanding international relations theory helps countries build better relationships with each other.

Treaties and Alliances

Aid Effectiveness

Pretend you have a super special tool that helps you fix things around the house. But sometimes, you need to figure out the best way to use it so it works perfectly. Aid effectiveness is like figuring out the best way to use this tool to help people in other countries. It's about making sure the help we give really makes a positive difference.

Bilateral vs. Multilateral Treaties

Imagine you have a big project to do at home. If you work with just one friend, that's a bilateral project. But if you work with a whole group of friends, that's a multilateral project. Bilateral and multilateral treaties are a bit like these projects. They're agreements between countries to work together, either just with one other country (bilateral) or with many (multilateral).

Collective Security

Think of a team of superheroes who all promise to help each other if any one of them is in trouble. They watch out for each other, and if someone faces a big challenge, they all jump in to help. Collective security in international relations is like this superhero team, but for countries. They promise to come to each other's aid if any of them face a big problem.

Conflict Resolution

Pretend you and your friends have a big argument about which game to play. Instead of arguing, you talk calmly and find a game that everyone enjoys. That's a bit like conflict resolution - it's about finding peaceful solutions to disagreements or fights. In international relations, it's about finding peaceful solutions when countries have disagreements.

Consular Services

Imagine you're in a big adventure, and you have a special guide who knows all the secret paths and can help you if you get into any trouble. Consular services are a bit like having a guide when you're in a foreign country. They're there to help you if you face any challenges or need assistance.

Consulate

Think of a consulate as a special clubhouse for visitors from your school who come from other places. It's a safe and friendly place where they can get help, find information, and feel at home even though they're far from their own school.

Cyber Warfare

Let's say you and your friends are playing a game on the computer, and you find out that someone is trying to cheat and mess up the game for everyone. Cyber warfare is like a big online game, but some people are trying to do sneaky things to win or cause problems for others. It's like trying to keep the game fair and fun for everyone.

Détente

Imagine you have two friends who have been arguing a lot, but then one day they decide to sit down, talk calmly, and find a way to get along better. Détente in international relations is like that moment when countries who have been having disagreements decide to sit down, talk, and try to find ways to get along better.

Defense Pacts

Think of defense pacts like having a group of friends who promise to protect each other if anyone tries to cause trouble. They stand together and make sure everyone is safe. Defense pacts in international relations are like this, but for countries. They promise to help each other if any of them face a threat.

Diplomatic Immunity

Pretend you have a special shield that makes you completely invincible. You can go anywhere and do anything, and no harm can come to you. Diplomatic immunity is like this special shield, but for diplomats. It means they have special protection when they're working in other countries, so they can do their jobs without any worries.

Economic Sanctions

Imagine you're playing a game with your friends, and if someone breaks a rule, they have to sit out for a little while. Economic sanctions are a bit like this, but in international relations. If a country doesn't follow certain rules or behaves badly, other countries might stop doing business with them for a while to encourage them to do better.

Euroscepticism

Pretend there's a new game in town, and some of your friends aren't sure if they want to play. They're a bit skeptical about whether it will be fun or not. Euroscepticism is like this, but with countries and a special group they might want to join. Some countries might be unsure if they want to be part of this special group called the European Union, so they're a bit cautious about it.

Foreign Aid

Think of foreign aid like sharing your lunch with a friend who forgot theirs. You have plenty, and you want to help them out. Foreign aid is when one country helps out another country by giving them things they need, like food, medicine, or money.

Free Trade Agreement

Imagine if you and your friends decided to trade toys. You give your extra Legos to a friend who loves building, and they give you their extra art supplies because they know you love drawing. A free trade agreement between countries is like this, but on a much bigger scale. It's when countries agree to trade goods and services with each other without many restrictions.

Humanitarian Aid

Pretend there's a big storm, and some of your friends' houses got damaged. You and your family gather up extra blankets, food, and clothes to help them out. Humanitarian aid is a bit like this, but on a bigger scale. It's when one country or group of people helps out another country or group of people who are going through a tough time.

Humanitarian Intervention

Imagine if you saw one of your friends being treated unfairly or getting bullied. You step in to help and make sure they're okay. Humanitarian intervention in international relations is a bit like this. It's when countries step in to help if they see that another country's people are being treated unfairly or in a way that's not right.

International Law

Think of international law like a big rulebook that countries agree to follow. It helps make sure that everyone plays fair and treats each other with respect. Just like you follow rules in games to make sure everyone has a good time, countries follow international law to make sure everyone gets along well.

Non-Proliferation Treaty

Imagine if there was a rule that said only certain people were allowed to use special tools because they were very powerful and could be dangerous if used the wrong way. The Non-Proliferation Treaty is a bit like this, but for countries and very powerful weapons. It's an agreement that says only some countries can have these powerful tools, and they promise not to share them with others.

Peacekeeping

Think of peacekeeping like being a really good mediator between friends who are having a disagreement. You help them talk it out and find a solution that makes everyone happy. Peacekeeping in international relations is a bit like this, but on a bigger scale. It's when countries help other countries talk through their disagreements and find peaceful solutions.

Proxy War

Imagine if you and your friends decided to have a big water balloon fight, but instead of getting wet yourselves, you each pick a friend to throw the balloons for you. A proxy war is a bit like this. It's when two big countries have a disagreement, but instead of fighting directly, they each support smaller groups who fight on their behalf.

Regime Change

Pretend you and your friends are playing a game, but one player isn't being fair and is causing problems for everyone. You all agree to choose a new leader to make the game more fun for everyone. Regime change in international relations is a bit like this. It's when countries work together to help a country choose a new leader if the current one isn't doing a good job.

Security Council (of the United Nations)

Think of the Security Council like a team of superhero leaders who make sure everyone plays fair and safe in the big world game. They watch over all the countries and help make important decisions to keep the peace. The Security Council of the United Nations is like this superhero team. They work together to make sure everyone is safe and fair in the world.

Security Dilemma

Imagine you and your friends each have a special protective shield, but you're not sure if you can trust everyone to use them nicely. If you all put your shields up, it might make some friends nervous, even though you just want to be safe. The security dilemma in international relations is a bit like this. Sometimes, one country tries to protect itself, but it makes other countries nervous because they're not sure if it's for protection or something else.

Soft Power

Think of soft power like having a super friendly and kind nature that makes everyone want to be your friend. You don't have to use force or be tough – you just naturally make people like you. Soft power in international relations is a bit like this. It's when a country's kindness, culture, and helpfulness make other countries want to work with them and be friends.

Treaties

Imagine you and your friends making a promise to always share your toys and take turns playing with them. You all agree, and now you have an official promise to be fair. Treaties between countries are a bit like this. They're official promises where countries agree to do certain things, like trade with each other, protect each other, or follow specific rules.

Treaty Negotiation

Think of treaty negotiation like deciding on the rules for a big game you're all going to play. You talk about what's fair, what's not allowed, and how everyone can have a good time. Treaty negotiation between countries is a bit like this. They sit down and talk about the rules they'll follow when they work together.

Treaty Ratification

Imagine you and your friends have decided on the rules for your big game. Now you all shake hands and agree that you're going to stick to these rules. Treaty ratification is a bit like this. It's when countries officially agree to follow the rules they've talked about and decided on.

War Crimes

Pretend you and your friends are playing a game, but one person starts breaking the rules in a really serious way and hurts others. War crimes are like this, but on a much bigger scale. It's when during a big "game" called war, someone does something really, really wrong and hurts others in a way that's against the rules of humanity.

8

Political Activism and Movements

Activism

Activism

Think of activism like being a superhero for a cause you really believe in. Just like superheroes use their powers to make the world a better place, activists use their voices and actions to make positive changes in the world.

Advocacy Groups

Pretend your school has a club of students who really love helping others. They work together to plan events and raise awareness for important causes. Advocacy groups are a bit like this school club, but for grown-ups. They come together to make a big impact on issues they care deeply about.

Advocate

Imagine you have a friend who always stands up for what's right, even if it's not the popular choice. They're like a brave knight, fighting for fairness and justice. An advocate is a bit like this brave knight. They speak up and fight for what they believe is right.

Boston Tea Party

Picture a time when you and your friends were really upset because someone was being unfair. You decided to come together and make a big statement to show that you wouldn't stand for it. The Boston Tea Party was a bit like this, but in history. People were upset about unfair rules, so they took action to show their disagreement.

Campaign Trail

Let's say you're running for class president. You'd go from classroom to classroom, telling your friends why you'd be the best choice. The campaign trail is like this, but for grown-ups who want to be leaders of their city, state, or even the whole country. They travel around, talking to people and sharing their ideas.

Civic Engagement

Imagine your town is like a big puzzle, and everyone needs to work together to make it complete. Civic engagement is a bit like being a puzzle piece that fits perfectly into your town. It means getting involved, helping out, and making your town even better.

Civil Disobedience

Think of civil disobedience like a peaceful protest, where everyone sits down together and says, "We won't move until things are made right." It's like a big game of musical chairs, but instead of moving when the music stops, everyone stays put to make a point about something important.

Grassroots Movements

Picture a garden where everyone helps plant seeds and take care of the plants. Grassroots movements are a bit like this garden. They start small, with regular people coming together to make positive changes in their community. Just like a garden grows over time, grassroots movements grow and make a bigger impact.

Political Advocacy

Imagine you really love a certain type of book, and you want to tell everyone about it because you think it's amazing. Political advocacy is a bit like this, but instead of a book, it's about sharing your beliefs and ideas about how to make the world a better place.

Political Apathy

Let's say there's a big game happening, but some of your friends just don't seem interested. They'd rather do something else. Political apathy is a bit like this. It's when people don't feel very interested or excited about getting involved in politics or making changes in their community.

Political Dissent

Think of political dissent like having a different opinion about what game to play with your friends. You want to play a game you love, but they want to play a different one. Political dissent is a bit like this, but it's about having different opinions on important issues in your community or country.

Political Dissident

Imagine there's a big group of friends, but one friend always has different ideas and speaks up about them. They're like the brave explorer who's not afraid to go a different way. A political dissident is a bit like this brave explorer. They have different ideas and aren't afraid to share them, even if it's not the popular choice.

Protest

Picture a time when you and your friends all hold up signs with messages you believe in. It's like a big, peaceful parade to show everyone what's important to you. A protest is a bit like this parade, but it's a way for people to come together and share their opinions about important issues.

Advocacy Groups

Human Rights Watch

Think of Human Rights Watch like a group of superhero defenders, but instead of fighting bad guys, they fight for fairness and kindness all around the world. They keep an eye out for places where people might not be treated as nicely as they should be, and they work hard to make sure everyone is treated with respect.

Non-Governmental Organization (NGO)

Imagine a big treehouse where kids from different houses come together to make cool projects and help each other. An NGO is like this treehouse, but for grown-ups. They're groups of people who come together to work on important projects and make positive changes in the world, without being part of the government.

Special Interest Group

Pretend you and your friends really, really love playing a special game. You have a whole club just for that game, where you talk about new strategies and share tips. A special interest group is a bit like this club, but for grown-ups who really care about a specific topic or cause. They come together to work on projects and make a difference in that area.

Civil Rights Movement

Civil Rights Act

Think of the Civil Rights Act like a powerful tool kit that helps make sure everyone is treated fairly and kindly. Just like a tool kit has different tools for fixing different things, the Civil Rights Act has rules and laws to fix unfair treatment and make sure everyone has equal rights.

Civil Rights Activists

Picture a group of brave knights who wear special armor to fight for what's right and fair. Civil rights activists are a bit like these brave knights, but instead of armor, they use their voices, actions, and kindness to fight for fairness and justice.

Civil Rights Movement

Imagine a big team of friends who come together to play a game. They work together to make sure everyone gets a fair turn and no one is left out. The Civil Rights Movement is a bit like this big team, but instead of a game, they work together to make sure everyone gets fair treatment and equal rights.

Desegregation

Pretend there's a big puzzle, but all the pieces are separated into different boxes. To finish the puzzle, you need to mix and match pieces from all the boxes. Desegregation is a bit like this - it's about bringing people from different backgrounds together, so everyone can work as a team.

Integration

Think of integration like a big, colorful mosaic made of different tiles. Each tile is unique, but when they come together, they create a beautiful picture. Integration is a bit like this mosaic, but instead of tiles, it's about bringing people from different backgrounds and cultures together to create a harmonious community.

Nonviolent Resistance

Imagine you're playing a game and someone starts playing too rough. Instead of getting upset and playing rough back, you calmly and peacefully ask them to play more gently. Nonviolent resistance is a bit like this - it's a way to stand up for what's right and fair, using calm words and actions instead of force.

Segregation

Picture a school playground with different areas where kids are playing separately. One area is for games, another for drawing, and so on. Segregation is a bit like this, but in history, it means keeping people from different backgrounds separate, even when they want to play together.

Environmentalism

Climate Change Activists

Think of climate change activists like a team of nature superheroes. They work together to protect our planet, just like superheroes team up to save the day. These activists use their voices and actions to fight against things that harm our environment.

Conservation

Pretend you have a magical garden with beautiful flowers and trees. You want to take care of it and make sure it stays magical forever. Conservation is like being the guardian of this magical garden. It means protecting and looking after our natural world so it can stay wonderful for a long, long time.

Conservationists

Imagine a group of wise wizards who have a special love for nature. They use their knowledge and magic to keep forests, rivers, and wildlife safe. Conservationists are a bit like these wise wizards. They use their knowledge and efforts to protect the natural world.

Environmentalism

Think of environmentalism as being a superhero for the Earth. Just like superheroes use their powers to save people, environmentalists use their passion and actions to save our planet. They work to keep the air clean, the water clear, and the land healthy for all living things.

Green Initiatives

Picture a big treasure map that shows the way to a special hidden place. Green initiatives are like this treasure map, but instead of leading to gold, they lead to ways we can help the environment. They show us how to make small changes that have a big positive impact on our planet.

Sustainability

Imagine you have a magical bag of snacks, and you want to make sure it lasts for a very long time. You eat just a little bit each day so it doesn't run out too quickly. Sustainability is a bit like this. It's about using our resources in a way that keeps them around for a very, very long time, so everyone can enjoy them.

Feminist Movement

Empowerment

Think of empowerment like giving someone a magical cape that makes them feel strong, brave, and capable of anything. When people feel empowered, it's like they have this special cape that helps them believe in themselves and do amazing things.

Feminist Movement

Pretend there's a big team of superheroes, but they're all focused on making sure boys and girls are treated the same and have the same opportunities. The Feminist Movement is like this team of superheroes. They work together to fight for fairness and equality for everyone, no matter their gender.

Gender Equality

Imagine a seesaw where both sides are perfectly balanced, so no one feels left out or unfairly treated. Gender equality is a bit like this balanced seesaw. It means making sure boys and girls have the same chances to play, learn, and do anything they dream of.

Gender Stereotypes

Picture a box of crayons with labels that say which colors boys and girls should use. But what if someone wants to use any color they like? Gender stereotypes are like these labels. They tell people what they "should" do based on if they're a boy or a girl, but it's much better to let everyone choose what they love.

Suffragette

Imagine a big puzzle where a few pieces are missing. The suffragettes are like those missing puzzle pieces. They fought bravely so that girls and women could have a say in how things are done, just like boys and men do.

Suffragettes

Picture a group of determined friends who want to make sure everyone's voice is heard. The suffragettes are like these friends. They worked together to make sure girls and women could vote and have a say in important decisions.

Women's Rights Activists

Think of women's rights activists like superheroes who use their powers to make sure girls and women are treated just as fairly and kindly as boys and men. They stand up for what's right and make sure everyone has equal chances and opportunities.

Human Rights Advocacy

Advocacy for Vulnerable Populations

Pretend you have a team of super friends, and some of them have special powers to help those who need it most. Advocacy for vulnerable populations is like these super friends using their special abilities to protect and support people who might be facing tough times.

Amnesty International

Think of Amnesty International like a worldwide group of kind-hearted detectives. They search for places where people might not be treated fairly and they work hard to make things right. They want to ensure that everyone, no matter where they are, is treated with kindness and respect.

Dignity and Equality

Imagine a big playground where everyone gets to play the games they love, and no one feels left out. Dignity and equality are a bit like this wonderful playground. They mean treating everyone with respect, making sure everyone has a fair chance, and nobody feels left behind.

Human Rights Advocacy

Think of human rights advocacy like being a superhero for fairness and kindness. Just like superheroes use their powers to save people, human rights advocates use their voices and actions to protect the rights and dignity of all people, everywhere in the world.

Humanitarian Efforts

Pretend there's a big box of kindness and care that people send to places where others need help. Humanitarian efforts are like this box, but it's filled with things like food, clothes, and medicine, sent to help people who might be facing hard times.

Universal Declaration of Human Rights

Imagine a very special rulebook that says how everyone in the world should be treated - with fairness, kindness, and respect. The Universal Declaration of Human Rights is a bit like this special rulebook. It lists all the important rights that every person should have, no matter where they live.

9

Public Policy and Governance

Climate Change Policy

Green New Deal

Let's say you have a big messy room full of toys and books. The Green New Deal is like a special plan that helps you clean up the room, organize everything, and make it a really awesome and eco-friendly place to play. It's a bit like having a team of helpful friends who work together to make your room the best it can be!

Communications

Public Information Officer

Think of a Public Information Officer as a friendly tour guide at a museum. Their job is to show visitors around, explain interesting things, and make sure everyone has a great time. In a similar way, a Public Information Officer in the world of governance helps share important information with the public, making sure everyone understands what's going on and feels informed.

Demography

Census Enumerator

Pretend you're a detective on a mission to count all the different types of animals in a big zoo. You walk around with your clipboard, carefully checking each cage to make sure you don't miss any. A Census Enumerator is a bit like this animal detective, but instead of counting animals, they go to different houses and ask questions to count how many people live in a city or country. They help make sure everyone is counted and accounted for.

Economic Development

Economic Development Specialist

Think of an Economic Development Specialist like a superhero with a special power to make towns and cities even better. Just like superheroes have the ability to fix things and make them awesome, an Economic Development Specialist has the skills to help towns and cities grow and become even more wonderful places to live.

They work with local leaders to come up with smart ideas, like building new parks, schools, and cool places for people to enjoy. They're like the architects of making towns and cities as awesome as they can be!

Education Policy

Education Policy Analyst

Think of an Education Policy Analyst as a treasure hunter who looks for the best ways to make schools even more awesome! Just like a treasure hunter searches for hidden treasures, an Education Policy Analyst searches for fantastic ideas and strategies to help schools teach kids better. They explore different methods, like finding the best books, games, and activities to make learning super fun for everyone.

They're like the champions of making school a place where every student can thrive and learn amazing things!

Environmental Policy

Environmental Analyst

An Environmental Analyst is a bit like a nature detective. Imagine you're in a big forest, and you have a special magnifying glass that helps you see all the tiny creatures and plants. The Environmental Analyst uses special tools and knowledge to investigate and understand how we can take care of our environment, just like a nature detective helps protect the forest and its creatures.

They're like the guardians of nature, making sure our world stays healthy and beautiful for everyone to enjoy!

Globalization

Foreign Direct Investment (FDI)

Pretend you have a lemonade stand, and your friend from another neighborhood loves your lemonade so much that they want to be a part of your business. They give you some of their toys to help make the stand even better. This is a bit like Foreign Direct Investment, where people from different places invest in a country's businesses to help them grow and become even more successful.

Trade Surplus/Deficit

Think of trading cards. If you have more of one type of card than you need, you can swap them with your friends to get the cards you really want. This is a bit like countries trading with each other. When a country has more goods to sell than it buys, it's like having extra cards to trade. That's a Trade Surplus. On the other hand, if a country buys more than it sells, it's like really wanting specific cards and giving away a lot in exchange. That's a Trade Deficit.

Governance

Draining the Swamp

Pretend you have a fish tank at home, and sometimes it gets a bit messy with extra food and dirt. To keep the fish healthy, you need to clean the tank and remove the extra stuff. "Draining the swamp" is like giving your fish tank a good cleaning. In politics, it means getting rid of any unfair or corrupt practices to make sure everything is fair and transparent.

Political Dynasty

Imagine you have a big family with lots of brothers and sisters. Now, let's say one of your siblings becomes the leader of your family's club, and then their child becomes the leader, and so on. This is a bit like a Political Dynasty. It means a series of leaders in a family who take turns being in charge. In politics, it's when one family seems to always have members in powerful positions.

Health Policy

Public Health Officer

Think of a Public Health Officer like a superhero whose special power is keeping everyone in the city healthy and strong. Just like superheroes have the ability to protect the city from bad things, a Public Health Officer uses their knowledge and skills to make sure everyone has the right information and resources to stay well.

They're like the health guardians, making sure everyone knows how to eat healthy, stay clean, and get the right medicine when they need it!

Immigration Policy

Deportation

Pretend you're playing a game with some rules, and if someone breaks a rule, they might have to go back to the starting point. Deportation is like that in a way. If someone doesn't follow the rules of a country, they might have to go back to their own country.

Immigration Quota

Think of a pizza party where you have a certain number of slices to share with your friends. You can only invite a certain number of friends because you have a limited number of slices. Immigration quota is a bit like that. It's the maximum number of people a country decides to welcome each year.

Naturalization

Let's say you move to a new neighborhood and you really like it there. You make friends, learn the rules, and become a part of the community. Naturalization is like officially becoming a part of a new country's community. It's like getting a special membership card that says you're now a full member.

Open Borders

Imagine there's a playground where all the kids from different neighborhoods can play freely without any big fences or gates. Open borders are a bit like that idea, where people can move between countries more easily without strict rules.

Political Asylum

Pretend you have a friend who's been having a tough time at home and needs a safe place to stay for a while. You offer your home to them, and they can stay until things get better. Political asylum is like when a country offers a safe place to people who might be in danger in their own country.

Sanctuary City

Think of a special clubhouse where all the neighborhood kids can go if they need a safe space. A sanctuary city is a bit like that. It's a city where people who might need extra help or protection can go and feel safe.

Legislative Drafting

Legislative Drafter

A Legislative Drafter is like a wizard who helps turn ideas into magic spells. Imagine a group of people has an amazing idea for a new game, but they need someone with special skills to write down all the rules so everyone can play. That's where the Legislative Drafter comes in! They take the awesome ideas from the group and turn them into clear, fair rules that everyone can follow.

So, a Legislative Drafter is like the wizard who helps bring the game to life by making sure everyone knows how to play and have fun!

Public Goods

Common Resources

Think of a big playground with lots of toys. Everyone can play, but if too many kids try to use the same toy at once, it might get worn out or broken. Common resources are like toys at a playground. They're there for everyone to use, but we have to be careful not to use them up too quickly.

Non-Excludable

Pretend you and your friends are playing a game in your backyard. You can't really put up a fence to keep some friends out because it's an open area. Non-excludable means something that is open for everyone to use, and it's hard to keep certain people from using it.

Non-Rivalrous

Imagine you have a favorite song, and you listen to it as much as you want without stopping others from listening to it too. Non-rivalrous things are like that. You can enjoy them, and it doesn't stop others from enjoying them at the same time.

Private Goods

Think of a special toy that's just for you. You can play with it whenever you want, and it's yours to keep. Private goods are like that, things that belong to one person and not everybody.

Public Goods

Picture a big picnic in the park with delicious snacks and fun games. Everyone in the neighborhood is invited, and everyone gets to enjoy the party together. Public goods are like that, things that are available for everyone in the community to enjoy.

Tragedy of the Commons

Imagine a group of friends taking care of a beautiful garden. They all love it and want to keep it nice, but if too many of them pick flowers too often, the garden might get damaged. The tragedy of the commons is like a reminder to be careful and share things responsibly so they stay nice for everyone.

Public Policy

Policy Evaluation

Think of policy evaluation like a report card for a school. Just like your report card shows how well you're doing in different subjects, policy evaluation shows how well a plan or rule is working. It helps us see if the plan is doing what it's supposed to do.

Policy Goals

Imagine you're playing a game and you have a goal to reach a certain level or score. Policy goals are like targets or goals that we want to achieve when we make rules or plans. They help us know what we're trying to accomplish.

Policy Implementation

Let's say you're planning a big birthday party. You need to decide what kind of decorations, games, and food you'll have, and then actually set everything up. Policy implementation is like organizing and setting up a party, but instead, it's about putting a plan or rule into action.

Policy-Making Process

Pretend you're baking your favorite cookies. You have to gather all the ingredients, mix them in the right order, and bake them just right. Making policies is like following a recipe. It involves gathering information, discussing ideas, and creating a plan that everyone agrees on.

Public Interest

Think about a playground where all the kids get to choose which game to play. They might pick the game that makes everyone happy, even if it's not their personal favorite. Public interest is like looking out for what's best for everyone, even if it's not exactly what one person wants.

Public Policy

Picture a set of rules in a board game that everyone has to follow. Public policy is like a set of rules for a whole group of people or a community. It helps make sure everyone can play fair and have a good time.

Regulation and Taxation

Bureaucracy

Think of a school with different teachers, principals, and staff. They all work together to make sure the school runs smoothly. In a similar way, bureaucracy is like a system where different people work together to run a government or organization.

Collective Bargaining

Imagine you and your friends want to decide which game to play. You all discuss and agree on a game that makes everyone happy. Collective bargaining is like when groups of people talk and negotiate to come to an agreement, especially about things like wages and working conditions.

Conflict of Interest

Pretend you have a friend who really loves pizza. If they're in charge of picking what food to order for a party, they might choose pizza even if other people want something else. A conflict of interest is when someone's personal interests might get in the way of making fair decisions for everyone.

Debt Ceiling

Think of a money jar that can only hold a certain amount of coins. Once it's full, you can't add any more. The debt ceiling is like a limit set on how much money a government can borrow. It's like saying, "Okay, we've filled the money jar, we can't borrow more right now."

Deficit

Picture a piggy bank where you put your allowance. If you take out more money than you put in, you'll have less in your piggy bank. A deficit is when a government spends more money than it collects in a certain period, like a year.

Economic Downturn

Imagine a roller coaster ride at an amusement park. When the ride goes down, it's a bit bumpy and not as fun. An economic downturn is like when the economy takes a bit of a bumpy ride and things aren't going as smoothly as usual.

Economic Policy

Think about a plan for a big birthday party. You decide how many balloons, games, and snacks you'll have. Economic policy is like a plan that a government makes to decide how to manage money, jobs, and businesses in a country.

Economic Recession

Pretend you have a savings jar and you're adding money to it regularly. If one day you can't add as much as you usually do, it's like a small recession for your savings jar. An economic recession is when the economy slows down a bit, like a little hiccup.

Economic Stimulus

Imagine you have a toy race car and you give it a little push to make it go faster. An economic stimulus is like a little push or boost that a government gives to the economy to help it grow faster.

Eminent Domain

Picture a game of musical chairs. When the music stops, one chair is very special and important. Eminent domain is like when the government needs a piece of land for something really important, like building a hospital, and they have the authority to use it.

Fiscal Policy

Think about a parent managing the family's budget. They decide how much money should be spent on different things like groceries, bills, and fun activities. Fiscal policy is like a plan made by the government to decide how to spend and save money for a whole country.

Foreign Intelligence Surveillance Act (FISA)

Imagine you have a secret club, and you want to make sure everyone is safe and playing by the rules. You might have some special rules to keep an eye on things. FISA is like a set of rules that helps the government keep an eye on things that might affect national security.

Freedom of Information Act (FOIA)

Picture a library where you can borrow books to read. FOIA is like a special rule that says certain information from the government can be borrowed or accessed by the public, so they can learn more about how things work.

Gross Domestic Product (GDP)

Think about all the things you have in your room - toys, books, clothes. If you add up how much they're all worth, that's like your personal "room GDP." Now imagine doing this for an entire country - that's the Gross Domestic Product, which is like the total value of all the things a country makes and does.

Gross National Income (GNI)

Let's say you have a big family and everyone pitches in to help with chores. If you add up all the allowances and money earned by everyone, you get the "family GNI." It's like looking at all the money earned by the people in a whole country.

Income Gap

Imagine you and your friends are all saving money to buy a cool toy. Some of you save a lot, while others save a little. The difference in the amounts you save is like an "income gap" - it's the difference between how much money different people make.

Income Inequality

Pretend you have a pizza and you want to share it with your friends. But some friends get much bigger slices than others. That's like income inequality, which means that some people get much more money than others, even though they're all working.

Income Mobility

Think of a ladder. Some people can climb up and down easily, while others might find it harder. Income mobility is like how easy or hard it is for people to move up or down in terms of how much money they make.

Income Tax

Imagine you have a big jar of marbles, and you need to give a few marbles to the jar keeper as a fee for playing. Income tax is like a fee you pay to the government based on how much money you earn.

Income Tax Bracket

Think about a ladder with different steps. Each step represents a different group of people who earn a certain amount of money. Income tax bracket is like which step of the ladder you're on, and it determines how much tax you pay.

Inflation

Imagine you have a magic wand that makes toys grow bigger every year. That means next year, you'll need more money to buy the same toys! Inflation is like when prices go up and money doesn't go as far.

Infrastructure Spending

Picture a big LEGO set that needs extra pieces to make it even cooler. Infrastructure spending is like buying extra pieces (like roads, bridges, and buildings) to make a city or country even better.

Inheritance Tax

Think about sharing toys with your cousins. Sometimes, if you want to keep a special toy, you have to give some of your allowance to your cousin. Inheritance tax is like a rule that says if you inherit (receive) a lot of money or things from someone who passed away, you might have to share a part of it with the government.

Interest Rate

Imagine you have a special bank where you save your allowance. Sometimes, the bank gives you a little extra money just for keeping your allowance there. That little extra is like interest, which is like a little reward for saving money.

Mandatory Military Service

Picture a big team game where everyone has to take a turn being the leader. Mandatory military service is like a rule that says everyone in a country should take a turn being part of a team to protect their country.

Monetary Policy

Think about a parent who decides how much allowance to give based on how well you do your chores. Monetary policy is like when the government decides how much money should be available in the country and how much it should be worth.

Monetary Union

Imagine a big group of friends who all decide to save their allowance in the same piggy bank. Monetary union is like when different countries decide to use the same money or have similar rules about money.

National Debt

Pretend you borrow some toys from your friend and promise to return them later. Until you do, you have a "friendship debt." National debt is like when a country borrows money and has to promise to pay it back later.

Nepotism

Imagine you're playing a game and you let your sibling win, even if they didn't really earn it. Nepotism is like when someone gives special treatment or jobs to their family members, even if there might be other people who are more qualified.

Political Patronage

Think about a club where the leader lets their friends have special roles, even if there might be others who want to join. Political patronage is like when leaders give special jobs or favors to their friends or supporters.

Progressive Taxation

Imagine you're sharing candy with your friends. The more candy you have, the more you share. Progressive taxation is like when the government asks people with more money to pay a little more in taxes to help those who have less.

Protectionism

Picture a big game where you and your friends want to make sure everyone has a fair chance to play. So, you create some rules to protect everyone. Protectionism is like when a government makes rules to protect its own businesses and jobs.

Public-Private Partnership (PPP)

Think about a school project where you and a friend work together to make something awesome. PPP is like when the government and a private company team up to make a big project, like building a bridge or a new school.

Redistribution

Imagine you're playing a game and you have a bunch of toys. If you notice one friend doesn't have many toys, you might share some of yours to make it more fair. Redistribution is like when the government helps make sure everyone has a fair share of resources.

Regulation

Think about playing a board game. There are rules you have to follow to make sure everyone has a fair chance to win. Regulation is like the rules that the government makes to make sure businesses and people play fair.

Regulatory Agencies

Picture a group of referees in a sports game. They make sure everyone plays by the rules and nobody cheats. Regulatory agencies are like referees for businesses and industries. They make sure everyone follows the rules.

Social Cohesion

Imagine a big puzzle with many different pieces that fit together perfectly. Social cohesion is like when people in a community work together and support each other, making everything fit together smoothly.

Sovereign Debt

Think about having a special toy that you promise to trade with your friend next week. Until then, you have a "toy debt." Sovereign debt is like when a country borrows money and promises to pay it back later.

Sovereign Wealth Fund

Picture a big treasure chest where you keep all your special toys and treasures. A sovereign wealth fund is like a special savings account that a country keeps to use for important projects or emergencies.

Tariff

Imagine you're in a trading card game and you decide to trade one of your rare cards for a friend's rare card, but only if they give you a few extra cards as well. That extra trade is like a tariff, which is a tax on goods coming into a country.

Tax Deductions

Think of a special box where you keep tickets from fun places you've visited. At the end of the year, you can use those tickets to get a special discount on something cool. Tax deductions are like special discounts on your taxes for certain things you've done.

Tax Revenue

Imagine you and your friends decide to save some money together to buy a big gift for your teacher. The total amount of money you save is like the tax revenue - it's all the money the government collects from taxes.

Taxation

Picture a big group of friends who all want to buy a gift for your teacher. Everyone puts in a little money to buy a big gift. Taxation is like when everyone in a country contributes a little bit of money to pay for things like schools, roads, and parks.

Trade Union

Think about a team of superheroes who work together to save the day. A trade union is like a group of workers who team up to make sure they're treated fairly and have good working conditions.

Universal Basic Income (UBI)

Imagine you have a tree that grows special coins every month, and everyone in your family gets some coins to use. UBI is like when everyone in a country gets a little bit of money from the government to help them with their basic needs.

Regulatory Compliance

Regulatory Affairs Specialist

Think of a big playground with lots of different games to play. Each game has its own rules to follow. The Regulatory Affairs Specialist is like the person who knows all the rules for every game and helps make sure everyone plays by them. They're like the expert who keeps everything fair and safe on the playground.

Social Services

Social Worker (Government Agency)

Alright, imagine you're at school and you're having a tough time with something, like maybe you're feeling a bit sad or you're having a hard time with your homework. Now, think of a really kind teacher who's always there to help and make things better. A Social Worker in a government agency is like that super caring teacher, but for grown-ups. They're there to listen, support, and find ways to make things better for people who might be going through a tough time. They're like a friendly guide who helps families and individuals when they need it most.

Urban Planning

City Planner

Alright, let's pretend you're building an awesome Building Block city. You have all these colorful blocks and little cars, and you want to arrange them in the coolest way possible. Now, think of a City Planner like the master Building Block builder. They're the ones who decide where to put the roads, parks, buildings, and even where the coolest playgrounds should go! They make sure everything fits together just right, so the city is a fun and safe place for everyone to live and play.

10

Contemporary Issues in Politics

Civil Liberties

Militarization of Police

Alright, let's pretend we're playing a game of cops and robbers. In this game, the police have some really cool gadgets and tools to catch the robbers, like walkie-talkies, handcuffs, and maybe even a police car. Now, imagine if the police started using really big and powerful tools, like tanks and super tough armor. It might seem like a fun way to play the game, but in real life, it can be a bit too much. The Militarization of Police is when the police start using really, really powerful equipment that's more like something you'd see in a superhero movie. It's important to find a balance so everyone feels safe and protected without feeling like they're in an action movie all the time.

Climate Change Policy

Adaptation and Mitigation

Okay, imagine you're playing a game and suddenly, the rules change. You have to come up with new strategies to keep winning. That's a bit like what Adaptation and Mitigation mean in climate change.

Adaptation is like changing your game plan when things around you start to shift. It's like when you're playing a board game, and someone adds a new rule. You have to think quickly and adjust your moves to stay in the game.

Mitigation is more like preventing the game from getting too tricky in the first place. It's like making sure everyone agrees on the rules before you start playing. This way, everyone knows what to expect, and it's fair for everyone.

Carbon Emissions Reduction

Think of carbon emissions like clouds of smoky stuff that come from cars, factories, and other things that use a lot of energy. Imagine if we could make those clouds smaller. It's a bit like when you blow up a balloon, but then you let the air out slowly. The balloon gets smaller, just like we want the clouds of smoky stuff to get smaller. That's what Carbon Emissions Reduction is all about.

Climate Agreements

Okay, picture this: You and your friends want to play a big game together, but you need to agree on the rules first. So, you all sit down and talk about what's fair and what's not. Climate Agreements are a bit like that, but on a much bigger scale. Countries from all around the world get together and agree on rules to help take care of our planet.

Environmental Regulations

Imagine you're playing a game, and there are some important rules to follow. Maybe you can't move your game piece a certain way, or you have to take turns. These rules make sure everyone has a fair chance to play. Environmental regulations are like rules for how we take care of our planet. They tell us what we can and can't do to make sure we're being kind to the Earth.

Green Energy Initiatives

Think about all the different ways we get energy, like from the sun, wind, and water. Now, imagine if we tried to use these kinds of energy more often, instead of things like coal or oil that can be harmful to the planet. It's like choosing to play with toys that don't need batteries, so we're not using up as much power. Green Energy Initiatives are all about finding and using energy sources that are good for the Earth.

Cybersecurity and National Security

Cyber Resilience

Okay, think about your favorite toy. Sometimes, it might get a little scratched or bumped, but it's tough and can still work perfectly. That's a bit like being cyber resilient. It means being strong and smart when it comes to using computers and the internet. So, even if there are some tricky things out there, you can handle them like a pro.

Cyber Threats

Picture this: You're the guardian of a secret treasure, and some sneaky pirates want to take it. These pirates are like cyber threats—they're trying to sneak into our computers and cause trouble. But don't worry! We have some super smart guards (like special software and experts) who work hard to protect our treasure from these sneaky pirates.

Cybersecurity

Alright, let's pretend you have a super cool clubhouse with a special secret knock to get in. Only you and your trusted friends know the knock. Cybersecurity is a bit like having a special lock and secret code for your computer. It keeps out anyone who shouldn't be in there, just like your clubhouse.

Information Warfare

Imagine you're in a big game where the players use words and messages to win. But some players might try to trick others with tricky words. Information warfare is a bit like that game. It's when people try to use words, pictures, or messages in sneaky ways to gain an advantage. But just like in the game, we have clever strategies to spot those tricks and make sure we're getting the right information.

National Security

Alright, let's pretend we're all part of a super cool secret club. Our job is to keep our clubhouse, and everything around it, safe and sound. National security is a bit like that, but for a whole country! It's about making sure our country is safe from any kind of harm, whether it's from inside or outside. We have special teams who work day and night to make sure everything's A-OK.

Security Measures

Okay, think of your house. You have locks on the doors and maybe an alarm system to keep it safe, right? Well, that's like having security measures for computers and important information. It's a bunch of special tricks and tools that help keep everything secure and protected.

Remember, just like you have grown-ups who look out for you, there are really smart people who work hard to keep our computers and information safe. So, even though there are some tricky things out there, we've got a team of experts making sure we're all safe and sound!

Global Security

Autonomous Weapons

Alright, let's pretend you have a really smart robot friend who helps you with your chores. You tell it what needs to be done, and it does it all by itself. Now, imagine if some people made super strong robots that can make decisions on their own, like when to fight or do things that might not be good. That's kind of like autonomous weapons. They can make choices without people telling them what to do, which can be a bit tricky.

Civil War

Picture this: you have a big group of friends, but some of them start having disagreements and don't want to play together anymore. So, they split up into different teams. It's like having a game where everyone isn't on the same side anymore. That's what happens in a civil war. Instead of playing games, though, it's about big, important decisions in a country, and it can be a very serious and sad situation.

Human Trafficking

Let's say you have a friend who really loves collecting toys, and sometimes they trade toys with other friends. But imagine if someone tries to take away your friend and make them trade toys without wanting to. That's what happens with human trafficking, but with people instead of toys. It's when some very bad people try to force others to do things they don't want to do.

It's really, really wrong, and we all work together to stop it.

Military Industrial Complex

Alright, think of a big team that makes lots of toys, like action figures, toy cars, and planes. Now, pretend this team is so good at making these toys that sometimes they make too many. So, they might want to sell them even if people don't really need them. That's kind of like the military industrial complex. It's when the people who make things for the military might want to make more and more, even when there isn't a big need for them.

War on Terror

Okay, let's pretend there are some not-so-nice imaginary creatures causing trouble in your neighborhood. You and your friends want to make sure they don't bother anyone anymore, so you work together to stop them. The War on Terror is kind of like that, but with grown-ups. It's when they work really hard to keep everyone safe from some really, really bad people who want to do very harmful things. They work together to stop them from causing trouble.

Globalization

Migrant Crisis

Okay, let's pretend you have a big picnic, and lots of your friends want to come over. But, imagine if so many friends showed up that your house started to feel really, really crowded. It might be hard to find enough space for everyone to sit and enjoy the picnic. That's kind of like a migrant crisis. Sometimes, in different parts of the world, there are so many people moving from one place to another that it can be a bit overwhelming for everyone.

Refugee Crisis

Imagine you and your family live in a big, safe castle, but there's a dragon outside that's scaring everyone. So, some families from nearby villages come to your castle because it's the safest place they know. Your family welcomes them in and shares your castle. That's kind of like a refugee crisis. In the world, there are sometimes very scary situations in certain places, and families have to leave their homes to find safety somewhere else. They become refugees, and they need help finding new safe places to live.

Identity Politics

Advocacy for Marginalized Groups

Alright, let's say you and your friends are playing a game, and everyone wants to join in and have fun. But, there's a rule that only certain players get to choose the games and make the rules. That doesn't seem very fair, right? Advocacy for marginalized groups is like making sure everyone gets a turn to choose and make the rules so that everyone feels included and has a chance to have fun.

Affirmative Action

Imagine you're picking teams for a big game, but some of your friends have never played before and might need a little extra help to get better. Affirmative action is like giving those friends a boost so they have a better chance to join in and play just like everyone else.

Apartheid

Think of a huge playground where all the kids can play together except some kids are told they can only use one part of the playground and can't go where they want. That wouldn't be fair or fun, right? Apartheid was a really unfair rule that said some people couldn't do the same things as others, just because of the way they looked or where they came from.

Ethnic Cleansing

Alright, imagine there's a big puzzle with lots of different pieces, but someone comes along and decides they only want certain colors in the puzzle and they take out all the rest. That's kind of like ethnic cleansing, but instead of a puzzle, it's about people, and it's really, really unfair and mean.

Identity Politics

Picture a big party where everyone's wearing different costumes to show who they are and what they like. Sometimes, people talk about the costumes they wear and how they relate to the other costumes. That's a bit like identity politics. It's when people talk about who they are and what's important to them, especially in politics, to make sure everyone's ideas and needs are heard and respected.

Inclusivity

Think about a big clubhouse where all your friends can come in and have fun, no matter what games they like or how they look. That's what inclusivity is all about – making sure everyone feels welcome and comfortable, just like they belong.

Institutionalized Racism

Okay, let's say there's a super long race, but some people start way ahead and others start really far behind, even though they're just as fast. That wouldn't be fair, right? Institutionalized racism is when rules and systems in a place make it harder for some people to succeed, just because of their race. It's like starting the race with a big disadvantage.

Intersectionality

Imagine you have a big box of crayons, and each crayon is a different color. But what if you have a crayon that's not just one color, but a mix of two or even more? That crayon is like you, with different parts that make you who you are. Intersectionality is about understanding that people have lots of different parts that make up who they are, like their race, gender, and interests, and all of those things are important.

Political Mobilization

Alright, let's say you and your friends want to have a really fun party, but you need to invite everyone and make sure they all know when and where it is. So, you start telling everyone and making plans to get them all excited. That's kind of like political mobilization. It's about getting people excited and ready to join in and make a difference in the world.

Safe Spaces

Think about your bedroom – it's your special place where you feel really comfortable and safe. Safe spaces in the world are kind of like that. They're places where everyone can go and feel comfortable being themselves, without worrying about being treated badly or feeling left out.

Separatism

Alright, let's pretend there's a big play area, but some kids want to have their own special corner with toys they really love. They still like playing with the other kids, but they also want their own special space. That's kind of like separatism. It's when some groups of people want to have their own spaces where they can celebrate who they are and what they believe in, while still being part of the bigger group.

Social Identity

Think about being part of a club where everyone wears a special badge to show they're a member. That badge is like your social identity – it shows the groups you belong to and the things that are important to you. It's what makes you, you!

Remember, just like in games, it's really important to treat everyone fairly and kindly, no matter what badges they wear or how they look. That way, everyone can have fun and feel included!

Polarization

Bridging the Divide

Think of a big river that separates two sides of a town. Sometimes, people on one side have different ideas or opinions than people on the other side. "Bridging the divide" is like building a strong, safe bridge so that everyone can talk and share their ideas. It helps them understand each other better and work together, just like good teamwork in a game!

Confirmation Bias

Imagine you have a favorite kind of ice cream, like chocolate. If someone offers you vanilla, you might say, "No, thanks. I know I like chocolate more." That's a bit like confirmation bias. It's when we tend to believe things that match what we already think. But sometimes, it's good to try new flavors (or new ideas) to see if we might like them!

Disinformation

You know how in a game of telephone, a message can get mixed up when it's passed along? Well, disinformation is a bit like that, but on purpose! It's when someone tells a story that isn't true, and it spreads around like a rumor. It's important to always check if the information you hear is from a trusted source.

Echo Chambers

Imagine you're in a big room with walls that make your voice bounce back to you. When you talk, it sounds like a big echo. In a way, the internet can be like that. Sometimes, we mostly hear from people who think just like us. It's good to step out of the echo chamber and hear different perspectives too!

Partisanship

Think of a big soccer game where two teams really want to win. Each team has its own fans cheering loudly. In politics, partisanship is when people strongly support one group or party, like being a super fan. It's good to cheer for your team, but it's also important to remember to be fair and listen to other ideas.

Political Divide

Picture a big puzzle with two different pictures on each side. The line in the middle keeps the two sides separate. In politics, the political divide is when people have very different ideas and it feels like they're on opposite sides. It's like trying to put together a puzzle where the pieces don't quite fit!

Political Polarization

Imagine a thermometer that shows how hot or cold something is. In politics, polarization means the "temperature" of opinions is really high. Some people might have very hot opinions, and others might have very cold opinions. Finding a way to make the temperature just right can help people work together better.

Populism

Anti-Establishment

Think of the "establishment" like the big kids in the school who make the rules. Now imagine some students saying, "We want to play our own games!" That's being anti-establishment—it means they want to do things their own way.

Mass Appeal

Picture a big pizza party where everyone gets to choose their favorite toppings. If a pizza has mass appeal, it means lots of people really like it because it has something for everyone, just like a super fun party!

Political Rhetoric

Okay, so sometimes in arguments, people use really fancy words to make their point. Imagine it's like telling a story, but sometimes they might stretch the truth a little to make their side sound better. That's what we call political rhetoric!

Populism

Let's pretend there's a big game of tag, and someone says, "Let's play the way most people like!" That's a bit like populism—it's when leaders want to do things the way most people want.

Populist Leaders

Think about a school where a student becomes really popular because they know what games everyone likes to play. Populist leaders are a bit like that— they're good at understanding what most people want.

Populist Policies

Imagine if a school made rules that everyone really liked, like having extra recess time or more fun subjects. Those would be populist policies—rules that are super popular with everyone!

<h1 style="text-align:center">11</h1>

Public Safety and Law Enforcement

Animal Control

Animal Control Officer

Think of an animal control officer like a guardian for pets and wild animals. They're a bit like the superheroes who look out for animals in our neigh-borhoods. Just like a lifeguard watches over swimmers in a pool, an animal control officer watches over animals, making sure they're safe and well taken care of. They're the ones who help lost pets find their way back home and assist animals in need. They're like the friendly neighborhood protectors of animals!

Code Enforcement

Building Inspector

A building inspector is like a superhero detective for houses and buildings. Just like a detective looks for clues to solve a mystery, a building inspector looks for clues to make sure buildings are safe and follow all the rules. They wear a special "inspector's hat" and use special tools to check if everything is in order. It's a bit like a chef making sure all the ingredients are just right before cooking a delicious meal. The building inspector makes sure homes and buildings are safe places for everyone to enjoy!

Emergency Management

Emergency Management Director

An Emergency Management Director is like the captain of a ship in a storm. Just like a captain steers the ship and makes sure everyone on board is safe, an Emergency Management Director takes charge during emergencies like big storms or other disasters. They have a special plan (like a map) and make sure everyone knows what to do to stay safe. It's a bit like a superhero leader, making sure everyone has a plan to stay out of trouble when things get tough. The Emergency Management Director helps keep everyone safe and sound!

Environmental Protection

Environmental Conservation Officer

An Environmental Conservation Officer is like a guardian of nature. Imagine they're like the superheroes of the forest and rivers! Just like a lifeguard watches over the swimming pool to keep everyone safe, an Environmental Conservation Officer looks after nature and makes sure everything is in balance. They make sure people don't harm the plants and animals, just like a lifeguard makes sure everyone follows the pool rules. They help keep our environment healthy and happy!

Fire and Emergency Services

Emergency Medical Technician (EMT)

An Emergency Medical Technician, or EMT, is like a medical superhero who comes to the rescue when someone is hurt or sick. They're a bit like magical healers! Imagine you're playing a game, and when one of the characters gets hurt, a special healer rushes in with potions and spells to make them feel better. That's what an EMT does in real life. They come quickly to help and bring special tools and knowledge to make people feel better until they can get to the hospital.

Fire Chief

A Fire Chief is like the leader of a team, just like the captain of a sports team. Think about a soccer team. The coach plans the strategies, but the captain on the field helps everyone work together and makes sure they're all doing their best. The Fire Chief is like the captain of the firefighters. They lead the team to put out fires and make sure everyone stays safe.

Firefighter

A firefighter is like a brave knight in shining armor, but instead of fighting dragons, they fight fires! Imagine a castle with a dragon nearby. The knight rushes in with a shield and sword to protect the castle. Firefighters do the same thing, but instead of swords, they have hoses and special gear to put out fires and save people.

Paramedic

A paramedic is like a medical superhero who can help people in really tricky situations. Imagine you're playing a game and someone gets hurt in a place that's hard to reach, like up a tall tower. The paramedic is the one who knows how to climb up and rescue them! They have special skills and tools to help people, even when it's not easy to get to them.

Law Enforcement

Constable

A constable is like a guardian of a small town. Picture a constable as the friendly neighborhood superhero. They're like a watchful owl, always looking out for any trouble and making sure everyone is safe and sound.

Correctional Officer

A correctional officer is like the keeper of a special castle for those who need a little time to think about their actions. Think of it as a bit like a time-out corner but much bigger! The correctional officer makes sure everyone inside the castle follows the rules and learns to make better choices.

Deputy Sheriff

A deputy sheriff is like the trusty sidekick of the sheriff, a bit like Robin is to Batman. They help the sheriff keep the town safe, a bit like how a team of superheroes works together to save the day.

Parole Officer

A parole officer is like a mentor for someone who made a mistake in the past but is trying to do better. It's like having a coach for life decisions. Imagine you're learning to ride a bike, and your coach helps you stay on the right path and make good choices.

Police Officer

A police officer is like a real-life superhero! They're like a friendly neighborhood protector who makes sure everyone is safe and follows the rules. They're a bit like a guardian angel, always watching over the town and making sure everyone is okay.

Probation Officer

A probation officer is like a wise guide for someone who needs a little extra support. They're like a helpful map showing the right way to go. Imagine you're on a big adventure, and you have a special guide to make sure you stay on the right path.

Sheriff

A sheriff is like the leader of the town's protectors, a bit like the captain of a sports team. Think about a soccer team. The coach plans the strategies, but the captain on the field helps everyone work together and makes sure they're all doing their best. The sheriff is like the captain of the law enforcement team.

State Trooper

A state trooper is like a guardian of the highways, making sure everyone drives safely. They're a bit like a traffic superhero, helping to keep the roads safe and making sure everyone follows the rules.

Park and Wildlife Management

Fish and Game Warden

A Fish and Game Warden is like a wildlife superhero! Imagine them as the guardians of the animal kingdom. They're a bit like the lifeguards at a swimming pool, but instead of watching over people, they keep an eye on animals in the wild, making sure they're safe and sound.

Park Ranger

A Park Ranger is like the friendly explorer of a big, beautiful forest or park. Think of them as the expert adventurers who know all the secret paths and hidden treasures. They're a bit like a tour guide, showing visitors all the amazing sights and teaching them about the wonders of nature.

Public Health and Safety

Health Inspector

A Health Inspector is like a cleanliness superhero! Imagine them as the protectors of places where we eat and play. They're a bit like the referees in a game, making sure everyone follows the rules to keep everyone healthy and happy. Just like a coach trains a team, a Health Inspector helps restaurants and places stay in tip-top shape for all of us. They're like the guardian angels of our well-being!

Public Safety Communications

911 Dispatcher

A 911 Dispatcher is like the hero on the other end of the line when you're playing a game of "Help, I need it now!" Imagine you're playing a big adventure game, and there's a special friend you can call who knows exactly what to do in any situation. They're like the expert guide who helps you navigate through the challenges and makes sure help gets to you as fast as possible. They're the real-life superheroes who are always ready to assist when there's an emergency!

Search and Rescue

Search and Rescue Coordinator

A Search and Rescue Coordinator is like the captain of a special team of superheroes. Imagine you're playing a game with your friends, and you need to find all the hidden treasures in a huge playground. The Search and Rescue Coordinator is like the leader who gives everyone a specific job to do. They make sure everyone knows where to look and how to work together to find the treasures safely and quickly. They're like the wise leader who brings everyone together for a successful adventure!

Traffic Enforcement

Traffic Enforcement Officer

A Traffic Enforcement Officer is like a rule keeper on the road, kind of like a referee in a sports game. Imagine you're playing a game of soccer with your friends, but there are a few special rules you all need to follow to play safely. The referee makes sure everyone plays fair and follows the rules. In the same way, a Traffic Enforcement Officer makes sure everyone on the road follows the traffic rules to keep everyone safe. They wear a special uniform and use signals, just like a referee does in a game, to make sure everything runs smoothly. They help make sure our roads are safe and everyone gets where they need to go without any problems!

12

Conclusion

Congratulations, Awesome Learner!

You did it! You've explored the fascinating world of politics and government, and now you know all sorts of important stuff. From elections to laws, and from leaders to policies, you've learned it all.

Remember, knowledge is a superpower. The more you understand about how things work, the better you can make the world around you. Even though you're still a kid, you have the ability to be a positive force in your community.

Keep asking questions and keep learning. You're on a path to becoming a smart and informed citizen, and that's a big deal! So whether you want to talk about politics with your friends, impress your teachers, or just satisfy your own curiosity, you're totally ready.

And guess what? You're not alone. There are tons of other kids out there who are learning about this stuff too. Together, you can make a real difference in the world.

So go ahead, be curious, be brave, and keep being awesome! We're cheering you on every step of the way.

Big high-fives and a super big thank you for joining us on this awesome learning adventure!

-Aristotle

* * *

We would love to hear from **all of you** who supported this book!

Your **positive review** on *Amazon* would not only mean a lot to us, but it would also help other readers discover the book and embark on their own culinary adventure.

All it takes is just a minute to make a difference!

About the Author

The creative mind behind the '***Mind Shaping***' books, a line of literature devoted to improving lives through wisdom and insight, is **Aristotle**, a contemporary philosopher and genuine polymath.

Aristotle is not just an insightful thinker, but also a creative genius who is always coming up with new ideas and designs. His drive to explore new ideas is evidenced by his attempts to patent and market his inventions, which highlight his innovative spirit. Aristotle has always thought that information has the ability to influence how we live. He has set out on a mission to assist individuals in reshaping their minds and, as a result, their destinies. He has a plethora of experiences and a great grasp of life's complexities.

Aristotle has always been a source of wisdom, offering friends and students enlightening counsel that has changed their lives.Many owe his leadership and advice for helping them have better futures.

Aristotle ponders the nature of existence and shares his profound discoveries through his writings because he is passionate about learning what people really need. He thinks that a healthy mind may affect anything, including one's physical health, future prosperity, and beyond.

The commitment to lifelong learning shown by Aristotle is unmatched. His wide-ranging interests, which include project management, eastern medicine, real estate, and life insurance, are a reflection of his unquenchable curiosity. Aristotle speaks four languages casually and is a competent musician who plays the guitar, piano, and drums. His skills are as varied as his hobbies.

Aristotle has a variety of experience working in several financial institutions, including tech centers, bank teller positions, primary admin, and software engineering.

Aristotle is now keen to spread his knowledge by publishing "***Mind Shaping***" books. His books serve as a tribute to his dedication to assisting others in realizing their full potential by altering their thinking and setting out on a path to a better future.

Also by Aristotle

Discover the Secrets to Stress-Free College Success: Overcome Anxiety Effortlessly, No Matter Where You Begin...

Are sleepless nights and racing thoughts robbing you of your college dreams?

Tired of feeling overwhelmed by deadlines and exams?

Is social anxiety holding you back from making friends and enjoying college life?

Do you worry about your academic future, even if you've always been a top student?

Are you ready to break free from the shackles of college anxiety and seize success?

If you answered "yes" to any of these questions, then you're on the cusp of a transformative journey that will reshape your college experience. It's time to leave sleepless nights, overwhelming deadlines, and social anxiety behind. This book is your beacon of hope, guiding you toward a brighter future.

Now, let's dive into a fraction of the hidden treasures waiting to be discovered within the pages of this book:

Discover Your Fearless Superpower to **confront college anxieties**.

Unlock **Time Management and Financial Secrets** for a worry-free college experience.

Craft a **Masterpiece of your life** through the understanding of emotions, forging smoother relationships and academic ascension.

Unleash the power of **captivating and effective communication**, not just in academics, but in every facet of your life.

Master the Art of **Boundary-Setting**, taking back your personal space and fortifying your inner sanctuary.

Embark on an intriguing journey of **cognitive reframing**, silencing the thunderous negative thoughts that once held you back.

Begin an **empathetic odyssey**, extending compassion to yourself and others throughout your college adventure.

Set your sights on **achievable dreams** and watch your college path illuminate.

Immerse yourself in the enchanting practice of **mindfulness**, a soothing balm for your college anxieties.

Craft a **personalized study routine** that transforms you into an academic juggernaut.

Hone your **decision-making skills** into the precision tools needed to sculpt your college destiny.

Uncover these and much more towards conquering college anxieties.

"I'm too overwhelmed already; another book won't help."

Discover the book that's specifically designed to unburden you! Our guide isn't about adding more stress; it's about shedding it. It's tailored to ease your college journey, providing practical, time-tested strategies that can be implemented effortlessly. It's not just 'another book,' it's your ticket to a stress-free college experience.

"I've Tried Self-Help Books Before, and They Don't Work."

We understand your skepticism, but our book isn't just another self-help guide. It's a comprehensive roadmap tailored specifically to address college anxieties. With real-life success stories and evidence-based strategies, it's the difference you've been seeking.

"My College Anxieties Are Unique; No Book Can Help."

Your anxieties are indeed unique, but you're not alone. Our book addresses a wide spectrum of college anxieties, providing adaptable strategies to meet your individual needs. It's a resource that empowers you to create a personalized path to success.

"I'm too introverted; it won't work for someone like me."

Introverted or extroverted, our strategies are tailored for everyone. We understand that college anxiety affects individuals differently. Our book offers personalized approaches to suit your unique personality and preferences. It's not about changing who you are; it's about empowering you to thrive in your own way.

"I can't afford it; college is already draining my finances."

We understand budget constraints. That's why we've made this book an affordable investment in your future. Think of it as a small price to pay for a wealth of knowledge and guidance that can save you from costly mistakes and enhance your overall college experience.

If you're ready to transform your college experience and conquer your anxieties, then scroll up and click the "Add to Cart" button now!

Simple Guide to Stress-Free College Success: Thrive Socially, Excel Academically, and Conquer Anxiety
Our approach to addressing college anxieties is rooted in empathy and understanding. We with '*Mind Shaping*', prioritize positive, constructive methods to help students manage stress, conquer anxiety, and thrive academically. We believe that a supportive and encouraging approach is key to fostering resilience and success in the college environment.

Financial Terms Explained: Using Simple Analogies and Scenarios 10-Year-Old Kids Can Easily Understand
Dive into the world of finance with **Financial Terms Explained** by Aristotle. This engaging guide simplifies complex financial concepts for young readers (and adults alike). If you're looking for more educational and entertaining reads, explore Aristotle's other titles for a journey into various realms of knowledge!

Corporate Terms Explained: Using Simple Analogies and Scenarios 5th-Grade Kids Can Easily Understand
Ever dreamt of a delightful, immersive approach to acquaint your child with the intriguing world of corporations?

Are you in search of materials that resonate perfectly with your 5th-grader's learning style?

Do you find it vexing to locate accessible resources for teaching your child about the corporate realm?

Your quest concludes here! This book is meticulously crafted to render learning about corporations as exhilarating as playtime, brimming with invaluable insights.

Ultimate Idioms and Expressions Guide: 400+ Common Phrases Explained

Embark on a transformative journey through language with *"Ultimate Idioms and Expressions Guide: 400+ Common Phrases Explained."* This comprehensive guide unlocks the stories, meanings, and cultural contexts behind each phrase, offering invaluable insights for a deeper understanding of human communication.

Perfect for those seeking clarity on intricate idiomatic expressions, this resource is essential for anyone who has struggled to decipher certain phrases. It's an indispensable reference for learners of English as a second language, providing a solid foundation in understanding and utilizing colloquial expressions.

The Book of Flavors: A Deep Dive Into All Food Ingredients

The Book of Flavors is your exclusive gateway to a world of culinary mastery. Discover the hidden potential within each ingredient, gaining an edge over rival chefs. This is not just a book; it's your *secret weapon* in the pursuit of extraordinary flavors. Guard it well, for its knowledge is the key to culinary greatness.